Healing from
Codependency

HEALING
from
CODEPENDENCY

A Devotional with
Prayers and Practices
for Healthy Boundaries

Wendy Lehnertz, MAPC, LMFT

Zeitgeist • New York

I dedicate this labor of love to my daughter, Sity, and my birth son, Parker, the two most beautiful souls, who taught me the greatest lessons about God's love. May I inspire throughout this book just a measure of the Father's love for each of you.

Scripture quotations are taken from the (NASB®) New American Standard Bible®, copyright © 2020 by the Lockman Foundation. Used by permission. All rights reserved. (www.lockman.org).

Published in the United States by Zeitgeist™, an imprint and division of Penguin Random House LLC, New York.
zeitgeistpublishing.com

Zeitgeist™ is a trademark of Penguin Random House LLC
ISBN: 9780593886472
Ebook ISBN: 9780593885826

Book design by Will Mack
Author photograph © by Helen Hill Photography
Edited by Kim Suarez

Printed in the United States of America
1st Printing

CONTENTS

INTRODUCTION

Like many of you, I am a lover of God, a follower of Christ, and an avid student of the Holy Spirit. God called me early on, through my personal journey of healing from codependent patterns "to comfort those who are in any affliction with the comfort with which we ourselves are comforted by God" (2 Corinthians 1:4b).

Accepting God's course correction in my relationships—and the comforting way in which He did so—inspired me to my career as a faith-based therapist to countless couples, individuals, and families. I'm blessed with the opportunity to empower people to live interdependently with one another and free of the codependent burdens they were never intended to carry.

Pursuing God in my healing journey has taken me to humbling places, stripped away the striving, and left me to recognize and accept that I am human. I am made in God's image, "wonderfully made" (Psalm 139:14) and yet also given the freedom to choose between "life and death" (Deuteronomy 30:19).

When we intimately know and depend on our Creator, we can truly know ourselves, feeling solid and secure in who He made us to be. We can accept our imperfections while still aspiring to live by the fruit of the Spirit; allowing God to flow through us to love and to live within the healthy boundaries He has laid out for us. Healthy boundaries provide safeguards in self-control. Self-control is just that—control of *self*. We can control only ourselves, not others.

One of the greatest elements within our control is the freedom to earnestly seek God to work through us, in our humanity and in spite of it. I have many spiritual practices to help me do this—some days better than others, for sure—but one of the most consistent is a daily devotion of reading, journaling, and praying to inspire me to make real and practical steps of surrender to His Holy Spirit.

My dependence on the Lord is the key component to choosing healing, and most important, prayer is an opportunity to set my mind to God, to what is of spiritual versus cultural value. It's my way of coming to Him with *everything*! I do mean everything—from getting a good night's sleep to finding humility when my humanity wants to defend myself in an argument. Prayer is my time to allow His Holy Spirit to lead me, speak to me, guide me, comfort me, and oftentimes reassure me for the journey ahead.

God works in His perfect ways and perfect timing, as much as I might want to rush Him or argue with Him that my way is better. Although I have been hurt, betrayed, and disillusioned many times in my life, God always works it all out for my good (Romans 8:28). For instance, I would never have chosen for my mother to die when I was just nine years old. This left me and some of my siblings (although I won't speak to their personal experiences) to navigate our dad's grief over our own, attend to grown-up duties, and neglect our developmental needs for the purpose of pleasing or tending to others.

Yet I can honestly say, looking back, I see how God, over time, used my experiences to make me into the woman I am today. The struggle in my broken childhood helped me to seek and find true lasting love in the One my soul longs for! I pray that this devotional does the same for you.

ADDRESSING CODEPENDENCY WITH GOD AND FAITH

I'm sure we have all heard comments with underlying tones about "good Christians" being identified based on how much they sacrifice or serve others. Maybe we learn to downplay our need for other people's help to instead focus on more prayer or Bible reading. I'm not so sure we predominantly pick up on messages about the importance of both giving *and* receiving from one another.

As a whole, perhaps we have misunderstood what true Christian love really looks like, inadvertently encouraging codependent relationships by focusing too much on other people and not enough on our own soul-care. For instance, we may totally disregard the second part of "love your neighbor *as yourself*" (emphasis mine). We've prioritized other scripture that talks about not being selfish or too self-serving, somehow making "as yourself" seem bad and wrong. Meanwhile it's right there in three of the four gospels (Matthew 19:19, Mark 12:31, Luke 10:27) that we are to treat ourselves as we would our neighbor.

I am not encouraging that we follow the trends of current culture and swing too far the other way. Being self-absorbed and focusing on ourselves so extravagantly that we forget to look up from our phones to share a loving smile or conversation is not ideal.

I invite readers to find balance by seeking God first, self and others second. The dance of codependency can keep us in self-neglect and focused outwardly on what we can't control, or it can keep us emotionally isolated and believing we need only to be self-reliant to get through the day. Whichever side of the dance we find ourselves on, codependency perpetuates the absolute worst human condition—feeling alone and isolated. But no one is alone in God's embrace.

Interdependency and True Christian Love

Finding this more balanced pathway to true Christian love starts by surrendering to God's unconditional love. The only way we can love well is to allow God to love *through us*. He is the Potter, and we are the vessels (Romans 9:21) built to be solid containers to receive and savor His love, allowing it to imprint so strongly that it leaves a stain. I refer to this as "soul-care" or "self-love," as we truly surrender to accepting all that God intends so we can pour that love to others. But the story doesn't stop there, as we are purposed to receive God's love *from* others, as well (John 13:20).

I've had to practice receiving God's love, first and foremost, during challenging times. I remember getting into my car after an especially difficult day at work. My whole body vibrated with anxiety, and I immediately picked up the phone to call my husband, to have him calm me down. It was in those days of not having a charger cord in every nook and cranny and, lo and behold, my phone was dead. I had a ten-minute drive home, and the Lord said, *Come to me.* I imagined His loving gaze and embrace upon me, and by the time I got home, I was calm enough to ask my husband for a hug versus bursting in and venting about my day. In short, it was not his responsibility to make me feel better.

My dependence on God connected me with the soul-care and self-love I needed to help me be relational in a healthy way. Rather than being self-absorbed, I became interdependent with my husband by engaging with him about my day. I was able to confidently voice what I still wanted from my husband—physical touch—as well as ask him about his day and what he may have needed from me.

In kind, the healthy dependence Jesus had with the Father allowed a more interdependent relationship with His disciples. Jesus highlights the importance of continually receiving God's love, as He modeled frequently, going off to be with His Father to pray, rest, and be replenished (Matthew 14:23; Mark 6:46–47; John 6:15). In turn, how He loved, cared, and healed others was dependent on and empowered by His Father (John 8:28).

Jesus also illustrated the importance of interdependence by receiving provisions and support from His followers, providing us a picture of His inner circle of human support. Jesus, in part, relied on Peter, James, and John more so than the other disciples. Multiple pieces of scripture reference Jesus asking these three specifically to join him in prayer and to support Him (Luke 9:28; Mark 5:37; Matthew 26:36–46). In the garden of Gethsemane, Jesus even expresses anguish that they are not staying alert to pray with Him (Matthew 26:36–46); illustrating the myriad of healthy emotions that are part of interdependence.

I hope to inspire readers toward true Christian love by demonstrating the practicality of interdependence, which balances love for self and others, both fueled by God. True Christian love creates this amazing space in relationships where we have freedom and security to give and receive; to say "no" as well as "yes"; and to share in personal, spiritual, and relational growth.

Interdependence helps us identify our edges, where we end and the other begins, so we are clear on what we can control and what we cannot. We learn to actively listen and respect others, as well as ourselves. We take personal responsibility for our behavior. We maintain a clear sense of self as a solid valuable child of God, and we ask for what we need and want, while maintaining that we can survive when let down and disappointed. Interdependence leaves room for grace in relationship, because the truth is that no human can meet all of our needs—nor should they.

Breaking Codependency and Being Closer to God

Codependency, at its core, is really about trying to get *all* of our unmet emotional needs fulfilled through another human being. Unfortunately, we sometimes put too much pressure on others for our well-being when God is so ready, willing, and able to give to us if we were to just ask (John 16:24). What makes this most difficult is that sometimes we aren't even in touch with what we emotionally and relationally need.

For instance, between spouses, it may be scary or difficult to put words to something the two of them aren't even fully aware of, such as emotional needs. The idea of even having emotional needs probably has a vague ring of familiarity to it, but the specificity of those needs may be long buried. This can seem deceiving at times, because some people have no problem asking or expecting others to meet their *practical* needs, such as money, sex, food, or help with the laundry and kids. At the same time, other partners don't always even know how much they are taking in the relationship because they are too busy focusing on whether they have enough; not necessarily where it is coming from. Whereas the one wringing out the last bit of energy to *make* this person happy often resents that no one is doing the same for them. They long to be taken care of, for those needs to be met, while simultaneously resenting that they have to ask.

The good news is that we have the perfect parent in our Heavenly Father, who wants to give us all that we need (Matthew 7:11). He also wants to mature us to His way of relating and loving one another. Once we depend on our Father to sustain us, we experience tolerance when a partner disappoints, a parent is imperfect, a friend betrays, or a neighbor offends. We are also able to ask for relational needs that fuel love for one another and truly help us "love our neighbor as ourself."

BLESSINGS FOR THOSE SUFFERING

*There is always hope—you can walk away with that promise
every time you pick up this book. The hope is not in you or your
relationships but in the one true hope that anchors the soul*
(Hebrews 6:19).

For those who find themselves in self-neglect and focusing too much
on trying to get their needs met through other people, take these weekly
devotionals into your private prayer closet—let them be just for you! Allow
yourself to experience the gifts God has for *you* specifically. For some,
too much was expected of us during childhood; the focus may not have
been on our age-appropriate development but rather on what others
wanted, to help *them* feel better.

Sadly, these consistent experiences can create a hardwiring of self-
neglect and relying on others to know what is best for us versus trusting
God's Holy Spirit within. I encourage you to take the route straight to the
person God created in you. Consider your feelings and then what you
may need from God, self, and others—in that order. Appreciate how God
made you—you are enough! You are a very capable vessel with many gifts
and talents that need to be distributed with discernment. Allow God to
be your lover—"I am my beloved's and He is mine" (Song of Solomon 6:3).

For those who believe they need to be self-reliant and may not engage
toward others enough, take these weekly devotionals in with a childlike
humility of allowing God to be your Father and receiving His reparenting of you. Sometimes the innocent and carefree nature of childhood is
too brief, as children are somehow made responsible for themselves and
maybe even others before they are developmentally capable.

Such experiences as a child can result in a hardwiring of self-survival,
which may look self-absorbed at times, but pause and consider that God
can give you all that your soul needs. God wants to give you what you
may not even recognize you are missing: true interdependent connection with Him and others. Allow God to be your perfect parent, your Abba
Father (Romans 8:15).

HOW TO USE THIS BOOK

This book is meant to be experienced. In loving God (which includes loving ourselves and others), we want to do so with all of our heart, soul, strength, and mind (Luke 10:27). When we do this fully, there is a lasting imprint of positive change in our lives.

As such, this book is structured in two parts, with the first comprised of weekly devotionals you can read and savor with your thoughts, emotions, and maybe even a hot beverage and journal. Then, when you are ready, you can access more deeply how this devotional comes to life inside of you through recommended practices and exercises. These include guided imageries, movements, intentions, journal exercises, and behavioral challenges for you to try.

Here are helpful and practical tips before you start:

- First and foremost, be kind to yourself in this process. Acknowledge that God is more interested in the intention of your heart than in any one action.

- Set aside uninterrupted time to fully engage heart, body, and soul into these exercises.

- Splurge on a new journal or blanket (if budget allows) to bring a tactile sense of comfort to this time.

- Allow God to change you, releasing the expectation that you can change yourself. Notice and release habits of performance or striving to please Him—know that He is already delighted in you.

- Mindfully experience yourself without judgment. You will be surprised at how it helps you see others more kindly as well.

- Research shows it takes two to six months to build and maintain new habits and patterns. Make this short-term commitment, and reevaluate from there. Don't expect too much too soon and give up on yourself—God doesn't!

- Use a paraphrase or just a few words of the scripture presented to capture what God most wants you to hear. Release pressure to memorize every scripture featured.

- Share what you are learning about yourself with a trusted friend or family member. Repetition helps install new brain pathways.

- Follow through quickly on godly impulses, and watch them grow. Feeling inspired to ask forgiveness for an action you regret? A sudden urge to reach out to someone you care about before moving on with your day? Follow those impulses!

- Enjoy who God made you to be—fully human with faults and strengths, in need of a Savior who wants to inhabit and guide you.

- Finally, if you or someone you know is in an abusive relationship, please know you are not alone. You don't deserve to be treated this way and help is available. Reach out for help by contacting the National Domestic Violence Hotline at 1-800-799-7233 or by calling or texting 988, the Suicide & Crisis Lifeline.

PART 1

The Devotions

THINK ENOUGH (NOT TOO MUCH, NOT TOO LITTLE) OF YOURSELF

For through the grace given to me I say to
everyone among you not to think more highly
of himself than he ought to think; but to
think so as to have sound judgment, as God
has allotted to each a measure of faith.

ROMANS 12:3

The apostle Paul gives us permission to do what we rarely feel comfortable doing: *think enough of ourselves.* If we neglect to consider our own thoughts and feelings, we may act on what we think others want from us versus doing what God is whispering through His Holy Spirit. Sometimes we try to avoid conflicts by doing or saying what we think others want from us, perhaps not raised to consider we are valuable enough to have unique thoughts, feelings, and needs.

This was the case for Carol. Carol's upbringing left her hypervigilant around her father's moods. She focused on what might make him happy with her versus what she needed as a vulnerable child. Carol and I explored her childhood experiences to reclaim her feelings, beliefs, and needs. This helped Carol *think enough of herself* to engage in an interdependent relationship with her spouse instead of feeling responsible for trying to control what she wasn't able to control anyway: her husband's happiness.

Paul, in Romans 12, asks you to consider how God has made you—the thoughts, feelings, talents, and purposes He has instilled into your being. God does not expect you to hide or dismiss yourself but to appreciate your "enoughness" He has graciously bestowed. As my husband often reminds me in my journey, I don't have to be everything to everyone.

Practice for Strength and Healing

KNOWING YOU ARE ENOUGH (page 124): Sit mindfully with the Lord and experience His loving gaze upon you. Notice what He wants you to share with Him about yourself, and in turn, fully acknowledge and experience His interest in you.

Dear Heavenly Father,

Thank you for making me in Your image, and for bestowing upon me a unique personality with talents and gifts I can use for Your glory. Help me to see myself as enough, just as I am today. I appreciate that with You, guided by Your Holy Spirit, I can feel secure to make sound judgments.

In Jesus' name. Amen.

SETTLING INTO HIS SAFE SPOT

In peace I will both lie down and sleep, for
You alone, Lord, have me dwell in safety.

PSALM 4:8

This verse came to life for me when I visited Israel and witnessed a reenactment of how shepherds protected their sheep by building a protective barrier where they stood guard. To do this, the shepherd would first find a natural protection like a mountain front to serve as a secure backing to a pen they could build. Then they'd construct a fenced-in area around it, using wood and stone. The shepherd diligently stood guard with his staff outside the pen to ward off predatory attacks. It was such a beautiful visual of how God hedges us in spiritually and keeps our souls safe.

This verse is pivotal in creating a sense of security for those who find themselves on edge or feeling unsettled, especially in the quiet of the night. For those who experienced a lack of safety during childhood, as well as others affected by current circumstances, this verse can be like an adult security blanket.

On nights when my body just doesn't seem to want to calm, I often read this verse from back to front, taking my plea first to the Lord, the One who can make sure my soul dwells in safety. This invokes a visceral sensation of letting go of effort and allowing God to do His work in me. He offers me peace to lie down and sleep.

Practice for Strength and Healing

DWELLING IN GOD'S SAFETY (page 126): For this week's exercise, practice embodying God's truth that He can bring peace as you dwell in His safety.

Dear Heavenly Father,

You are an ever-present help in the dark of night when I need You most. As I will my body to dwell in You, O Lord, I can feel safe. Allow my body to rest in this peace, Lord, and to find sleep to refresh my soul.

In Jesus' name. Amen.

THE POWER OF INFLUENCE VERSUS THE URGE TO CONTROL

Therefore, though I have enough confidence
in Christ to order you to do what is proper,
yet for love's sake I rather appeal to you.

PHILEMON 1:8–9A

I love the level of respect Paul demonstrates in the form of true Christian love toward Philemon. I imagine Paul has a position of authority over Philemon, but instead of exercising demand and control, Paul chooses to utilize his influence by appealing to Philemon. It sounds like Paul knows he is in right standing according to Christian principles, but he exercises *a way of relating* to his brother rather than flexing power and control to prove he is right.

For those in leadership positions, and I imagine that is the majority of us—parents of children, bosses overseeing employees, teachers leading students—Paul has something foundational to teach. When we use the power of influence, we show a healthy respect toward others as heirs of God. *All* humans deserve to be treated and regarded with basic respect.

When we seek control or make demands of others, we break the cycle of loving relationship. No matter how "right" we may be about an issue, we run the risk of inviting resentment into the relationship. I often reference the time my husband wanted to make a wise financial decision for our family, but I wasn't on board with that decision for a while. Instead of exhibiting controlling behaviors toward me, my husband moved in with appeal—not the nagging kind, which is just a passive way of trying to control another person. Rather, his appeal was filled with greater conversations about his intentions, motivations, and desires for our family's financial well-being.

Practice for Strength and Healing

THE POWER OF INFLUENCE (page 128): Look at how you might apply positive influence to those in your relationship orbit and take steps toward using this to extend true Christian love.

> *Dear Heavenly Father,*
>
> *Thank You for showing me that we are all fellow heirs and that no one is greater than another. Help me to release the temptation to demand and seek control over others, even if it's for what is "right." Teach me to lovingly appeal with my power of influence for that which brings You glory.*
>
> *In Jesus' name. Amen.*

HUMBLE THYSELF

Therefore humble yourselves under the mighty
hand of God, so that He may exalt you at
the proper time, having cast all your anxiety
on Him, because He cares about you.

I PETER 5:6–7

I don't know which apostle you most relate to, but Peter is my guy. I envision Peter as an eager and sometimes overly confident leader. I could be wrong, of course, but regardless, he makes an excellent point in 1 Peter 5 when he addresses leaders and others given great responsibility. He refers to God's mighty hand to illustrate His strength that even the strong-willed need. He pleads also to their flesh by promising exaltation. *Others will admire you, don't worry,* he seems to be saying. The most captivating part of the verse is when Peter acknowledges that "He cares about you."

When we feel anxious or insecure, we might move toward seeking control instead of surrendering to His Spirit. Peter recognizes that it's key to humble oneself to God's love and care rather than trying to control others when we feel unsettled or worried. Human tendency may be to want to control certain elements outside of ourselves when we feel chaotic within. Fortunately, we are blessed with the ability and free will to consider our humble nature and to look at what we can control: casting our anxiety on God and feeling the warm embrace of His calming care.

Practice for Strength and Healing

TO CONTROL . . . OR NOT TO CONTROL? (page 130): This week, draw into your Heavenly Father's care to soothe you in your anxieties. Allow Him to speak to you about what you are able to control and what should be left to Him.

Dear Heavenly Father,

Thank you for being the strength I need in every moment. I can hardly fathom the love and care You have for me. My responsibilities and worries feel overwhelming at times, and I lose sight of You. Yet I can cast all my concerns on You alone, and You respond to me with Your everlasting love and care.

In Jesus' name. Amen.

PERMISSION TO BE ANGRY—BUT NOT TO SIN

Be angry, and yet do not sin; do not let
the sun go down on your anger.

EPHESIANS 4:26

Often in the dance of codependency, we feel we can't be honest about our emotions, especially anger. Paul speaks straight to our humanity here, wanting us to acknowledge our anger in a healthy way, without sin. He asks us not to lash out with verbal, emotional, or physical violence, or become passive-aggressive in expressing anger. Rather, he advises to put aside falsehood (Ephesians 4:25). So be honest about your emotions, and do so before bitterness takes root.

Be angry, and then pause. Allowing ourselves to identify, label, and feel anger can actually liberate us from acting out in sinful ways. God knows anger is an energy we experience in the body and that it needs to be discharged. Still, He warns us not to discharge it as a weapon.

One of two things typically happens when it comes to anger. We feel it too often and too quickly, letting everyone know it and leaving destruction all around us, *or* we hide anger and try to suppress it, allowing bitterness and resentment to grow more and more until we feel powerless.

What Paul is trying to help us get at is that anger is a normal feeling. Anger can help us have a voice and speak up for ourselves. Anger can energize us to set a boundary that enables us to take care of our needs. Anger might even inspire us to turn to Christ-centered solutions.

Practice for Strength and Healing

ALLOWING YOUR EMOTIONS (page 132): In this week's exercise, spend time exploring how you tend to process your emotions when you are angry. Take inventory of what you might be holding on to, and consider instead the boundaries you need to set for yourself.

Dear Heavenly Father,

Help me to release my anger in a way that is not harmful to others or myself. Guide me to put the correct words to my experiences, and give me the strength to be honest with others when I am struggling. When I feel weak, I will allow You to be strong in me.

In Jesus' name. Amen.

A FULL RANGE OF GOD-GIVEN EMOTIONS

Weeping may last for the night, but a shout of joy comes in the morning.

PSALM 30:5B

From sadness to anger, confusion to confidence, fear to security, despair to joy . . . God *intentionally* created us to experience a plethora of emotions. In fact, when we flatten or deaden ourselves to how life affects us in its ups and downs, we hinder our ability to experience the "joy that comes in the morning." Pure joy is the reward *after* a night of weeping.

God shows us repeatedly through scripture that this range of emotion is intended to bring us to Him in contrast to expecting other people to make us feel better. He promises to see us through those dark nights of the soul so we can rejoice with Him later. Many of the psalms sing about counting on God's deliverance. Psalm 31:7b–8 praises, "You have seen my misery; You have known the troubles of my soul, and You have not handed me over to the enemy; You have set my feet in a large place." I imagine this large place to be a space of freedom from emotional restriction.

Like with many adolescent boys, no one had walked Trent through healthy ways to handle disappointment and despair as a child, so he did his best and tucked his emotions away. He disconnected from his truth and just moved on. It was when his first son was born that he recognized he didn't feel much of anything in his life. Trent and I spent weeks reclaiming this part of him that had previously been cut off, reparenting him with God as his perfect parent. We spent time in his anger, sadness, and disappointment, digging up what had long been buried. Trent needed to be heard and felt by the Father, who could comfort him in his emotional needs. We were also intentional about mining the treasures of Trent's childhood—the beauty, joy, and delight. I still smile with gratitude that this earthly son found reconnection with his Heavenly Father.

Practice for Strength and Healing

PINPOINTING EMOTIONAL AND RELATIONAL NEEDS (page 134): You will practice with a daily feelings journal, bringing forth to God your emotions and trusting Him for the joy that comes. Whether in a day or months, in His divine timing, He will elevate your emotions.

Dear Heavenly Father,

I put my heart in Your capable hands. Please walk me through the darkness of my emotions so I can reach the morning joy. I want to trust Your deliverance and dance with You in Your glory.

In Jesus' name. Amen.

THE TRIPLE THREAT

For God has not given us a spirit of timidity,
but of power and love and discipline.

2 TIMOTHY 1:7

The above scripture invokes a very visceral sensation in me. It helps me stand up a bit taller to embody a humble strength that comes only when I surrender to His Spirit within me. What I love most about this trifecta of power, love, and discipline is that it feels like the perfect compilation of attributes to characterize confidence.

Confidence, different from pride, is really a surety that God lives in me and I can trust His Holy Spirit to guide me. Allowing Him to inhabit us with His Spirit of power, love, and discipline gives us this assurance, so we can relate in ways that are discerning and clear. This is important in relationship, so we can let "yes" mean yes and "no" be no. Communicating congruently with words, intentions, and body language is key to breaking the dance of codependency.

Upon studying the Enneagram—an ancient model of personality types as defined by a Christian mystic—I was relieved to learn I am not the only one who has noticed a phenomenon in which some people automatically say "yes" and others reflexively say "no." Responses seem to be related to people's focus on pleasing others or on hoarding their energies for themselves. The problem with reactive or automatic responses is that they may not be congruent with our true inner feelings and current needs. More important, such snap responses may not be consistent with the steps God is asking us to take to mature into greater relational health.

I used to say "no" before my partner or daughter had even finished a sentence. It was freeing for me (and certainly them) to learn that others have a similar tendency. I learned to accept my humanity, looking to God to slow my automatic response. I made room to accept His spirit of power, love, and discipline, and now I consciously discern whether a situation legitimately calls for a "no."

Until you learn to say "yes" or "no" with this type of integrity, consider active use of the word "maybe," and take time to pray and explore what God has called you to in any given moment.

Practice for Strength and Healing

FINE-TUNING YOUR EXPECTATIONS (page 136): To embody God's Spirit of power, love, and discipline, nonjudgmentally observe any automatic responses you might lean toward. Look to make shifts that align with God's Spirit, internally and externally.

Dear Heavenly Father,

Thank You for giving me Your spirit of boldness so I can lovingly be clear in my communications. Help me to recall this boldness when I need it and to grow in my discernment of Your callings. I desire to be a person of integrity, to the point where I mean what I say and say what I mean. Guide me, Lord, I pray.

In Jesus' name. Amen.

ALLOWING AND ACCEPTING EMOTIONS OF OTHERS

For if He causes grief, then He will have
compassion in proportion to His abundant mercy.

LAMENTATIONS 3:32

Often, we try to suppress our emotions, and if we are being honest, we sometimes attempt to block others' emotions as well. We might do this because no one taught us what to do with our emotions. In efforts to feel safe and secure in the codependence dance, perhaps we are lulled into believing that only if the other person is in a good mood or state of mind, then we can relax—yet we can deliberately choose not to absorb the tensions from someone else's moods. Allowing another person to dictate how we feel can be unpredictable, at best, and dangerous to our identity in Christ, at its worst. This dynamic places us in the powerless position of trying to manipulate someone else's feelings.

Tiffany's challenge, as an adult, was to allow God, whom she could accept was her one perfect parent, to help those she loved. Tiffany was always tempted to highjack the emotional process to which God had called her loved ones. Tiffany first needed to attend to her own inner world by reminding herself God was with her, that she could find safety in Him. She practiced healthy detachment in giving the appropriate emotional distance to allow God room to work in others. I reminded Tiffany that she could trust God to fill in the space while she reengaged from a more secure place within. She learned to show compassion, as God does, while noticing this is different than trying to fix someone else's emotion or make it stop. Compassion expressly acknowledges the emotion, allowing it to have space in the room.

When we highjack another person's emotions, we show lack of faith in God to comfort, exhort, or teach them. God needs you to stay out of His way so your loved one will come to Him independently. When we swoop in to fix or solve, we don't trust God's rightful plan to provide compassion and abundant loving-kindness.

Practice for Strength and Healing

GOD TO THE RESCUE! (page 138): This week you will practice being curious about others' experiences without becoming a firefighter trying to distinguish the emotions God uses to minister to them in His abundant loving-kindness.

Dear Heavenly Father,

Please help me to step back and let You rescue others from their emotional turmoil. I trust that Your love is abundant. I know You can provide for them and me at the same time. Help me to feel the safety and security of Your love in these moments. I'm blessed to be able to extend compassion to those I love. Thank you, God, that I don't have to provide a "fix."

In Jesus' name. Amen.

WEEK 9
FIGHT FOR ME, LORD!

Lord, you have seen the wrong done to me. Uphold my cause!

LAMENTATIONS 3:59 (NIV)

I love this cry for someone to fight for me! I love how Jeremiah expresses a need for God to rescue him. The boldness of holding *hope* that God will get him out of his oppression is admirable. That process may be long and grueling or short and swift, but the answer is clear that God wants to help us through *all* ordeals, even conflicts caused by our own hand.

In the dance of codependence, we might feel wronged or hurt by those who have the most access to our hearts. Lamentations 3:59 gives us permission to call out for a heavenly defense. This can help squelch the fires that fuel mechanisms of self-defense. I think of this scripture when I feel my character is in question because my husband, daughter, or friend misunderstood something I said or did. As I recall how intimately God knows me, more often than not peace settles in my soul. This gives me the centeredness I need to calm down and more clearly communicate what I intended, as well as try to better understand the other.

Trusting that God sees the *entire picture* supports me in knowing that He will see everyone through any conflict. Let's not downplay His amazing ability to come to all sides simultaneously and be "our help and our shield" (Psalm 33:20). Who else can do that?

Practice for Strength and Healing

BUT FIRST . . . YOUR EMOTIONAL WELLNESS (page 140): In this week's exercise we will envision God as our defender and embody the experience of surrendering to His just shield of protection.

Dear Heavenly Father,

Please, come to my rescue as needed. Some days, I'm too tired to keep going. When my spirit groans and I have no words left to fight, uphold my cause, Lord! Be my victory.

In Jesus' name. Amen.

NEEDS UNEXPRESSED MIGHT MORPH INTO MANIPULATIONS

You do not have because you do not ask.

JAMES 4:2B

James asks, "What is the source of quarrels and conflicts among you?" (James 4:1a). Although the majority of what he describes is potentially coming from "wrong motives" (James 4:3), I appreciate this simple statement he squeezes in there: "You do not have because you do not ask."

Many of us have been taught from a young age to not ask for what we need or want, for fear that we would burden or upset others. Quite the opposite is true. We burden and upset others when we try to manipulate a situation to covertly get our needs or wants met, instead of simply making the request.

Being the youngest of eleven, there wasn't much left for me in regard to my father's energies to parent. I learned rather swiftly to take care of myself. Years later, I finally learned that God never intended for me to meet all my needs alone.

I love that God gave me a safe enough spouse whom I can ask, "Would you be willing to . . . ?" He often is eager to please, but on those occasions when he has little in his tank, I am not left stranded. I have a Heavenly Father who wants to meet my needs and desires in perfect ways—sometimes through Him alone and other times within the fellowship of people He places in my life.

Practice for Strength and Healing

LETTING GOD TAKE INVENTORY (page 142): This week, put into practice this key element of interdependence by asking for what you need—from God and your loved ones. Grow in your ability to ask and trust that God meets you one way or another.

Dear Heavenly Father,

Thank You for giving me permission to ask for what I need or want. You teach us to not only ask You, but also to ask one another. You show us how to be in an interdependent relationship with a trinity of sorts: You, others, and myself. Although humans cannot always meet my needs, You surely can. Help me to trust in Your faithfulness.

In Jesus' name. Amen.

I SCREAM, YOU SCREAM, SOMETIMES WE ALL SCREAM

In the days of His humanity, He offered up both prayers and pleas with loud crying and tears to the One able to save Him from death, and He was heard because of His devout behavior.

HEBREWS 5:7

Jesus knew how to talk to His Father, with a blend of humility and authentic emotion. I recognize that we are not in the same position as Christ was when He was about to sacrifice Himself for the sake of our resurrection. However, we do feel sacrificed at times and so desperate in our need that all we can do is cry out. I appreciate the absolute assurance that we are heard, and when we have reverence to who we are crying out to, we in turn can hear His answers.

Reverence doesn't always mean our language is pretty. Reverence is a gut knowing that we are talking to the Most High, the Author of our lives.

So cut loose and cry out—don't hold back with God. He wants to lift and shift your burdens, so tell Him how you are hurting and what makes you angry. Expressing anger or despair in a nondestructive way, and not suppressing it, allows the emotion to be released so you don't stay stuck there. He is a strong God. He can—and will—even tolerate your angst when you are struggling to accept His plan for you. He wants to hear from you, His loved one.

Practice for Strength and Healing

EMPOWERMENT, COURTESY OF GOD (page 144): This week you get to practice being gut-wrenchingly authentic, as He knows what you are feeling and thinking anyway.

Dear Heavenly Father,

I am in such appreciation that You are big and gracious enough to hear my cries. Thank You for always understanding the depth of my emotional anguish. Sometimes I just want to scream and know that I am heard. Thank You for hearing me, Lord!

In Jesus' name. Amen.

BLAME-SHIFTING: THE OLDEST TRICK IN THE BOOK

And He said, "Who told you that you were
naked? Have you eaten from the tree from which
I commanded you not to eat?" The man said,
"The woman whom You gave to be with me, she
gave me some of the fruit of the tree, and I ate."
Then the Lord God said to the woman, "What
is this that you have done?" And the woman
said, "The serpent deceived me, and I ate."

GENESIS 3:11–13

When I read this portion of scripture, it seems almost comical in the blatant shifting of blame. Yet when it is happening to you, it is anything but funny. Whether you find yourself on the receiving or distributing end of this equation, blame-shifting is no joke!

When blaming others, we don't allow God to sit with us in accountability for our actions or choices. Blaming blocks our ability to perceive the reassurance and hope that He can help us correct our behavior. Many couples I counsel tend to point fingers when they feel a flash of shame or guilt hit their gut. Shame and guilt are emotions that can either sink us into self-loathing or lift us into true repentance. Blame is often an unconscious mechanism to avoid looking at our own contribution to a specific conflict or relationship dynamic. When feeling compelled to cast blame, it can be helpful to pause for a moment of introspection.

Blame, even when justified, serves no one. Blaming typically puts people into defensive mode, so instead consider extending curiosity and understanding, which is far more likely to inspire a show of accountability.

Practice for Strength and Healing

SHOVE OFF, SHAME! (page 146): Consider how you handle shame or guilt. Learn to rely more heavily on the truth that you could never make such a huge mess of things that you lose God's love.

Dear Heavenly Father,

I pray to stand on solid ground in absolute knowledge that You love me, even when I have behaved poorly. By standing in this truth, help me to have the courage to accept my missteps and seek repair, especially if I have hurt someone. I love You, Lord.

In Jesus' name. Amen.

A FRESH START EVERY MORNING

The Lord's acts of mercy indeed do not end,
for His compassions do not fail. They are new
every morning; great is Your faithfulness.

LAMENTATIONS 3:22–23

If you've read them, maybe you noticed that the first twenty-one verses of Lamentations 3 are pretty brutal—angst and despair, the sense of being unforgivable, crushed with shame and bitterness, feeling like a "laughingstock to all people." Do you relate to lows like these?

For me, the verse above is a breath of fresh air when I wake up after the previous day's struggles. Teasing out my responsibility in the struggle from the other person's becomes possible only when I start from the foundation that His compassions never fail. My angst matters to Him—because He wants to lead me to a solution.

I think about my former client Jim, who came into an early-morning session agitated about a conflict he had had with his neighbor the night before. Upon looking closer at this conflict and what needed to change to resolve it, I gently reminded Jim that God's faithful mercy and compassion was new for him on that day. God holds nothing against Jim or his neighbor. Recognizing that he could begin anew with a clean slate, Jim let down his defenses rather than clinging to emotions around the previous night's events. He was able to hit a reset button and take a more honest examination of his behavior and what he wanted to change. When we have this soft landing of God's love and mercy, we are much kinder to ourselves and hopefully more considerate of our neighbors.

What's beautiful about God's compassion is that it inspires us to live interdependently. I can rely on God's love to uphold me and my needs, while I take steps to reconcile my needs/wants with my neighbor's needs/wants for a healthy compromise.

Practice for Strength and Healing

LETTING GOD TAKE INVENTORY (page 142): You will learn how to receive the promise of new mercies every morning to give you the humility and strength to consider previous conflicts, including what you can take responsibility for and what you can't.

Dear Heavenly Father,

Your mercies and compassions are fresh every morning. Thank You, Lord. I know my sins and mistakes are forgiven. Help me move on in this day, without regrets dragging me down. I appreciate the opportunity to renew my relationships with myself and my loved one today.

In Jesus' name. Amen.

STANDING FIRMLY IN FAITH

Keep your behavior excellent among the
Gentiles, so that in the thing in which they
slander you as evildoers, they may because
of your good deeds, as they observe them,
glorify God on the day of visitation.

1 PETER 2:12

In the entire book of 1 Peter, he pleads with us to stand firm. He urges us to essentially hold a boundary for ourselves so that we will not be shaken by current culture trends and fashionable ways of living.

As young Christians, we may make radical changes to our behavior as we experience a significant shift when living in His Spirit after following our fleshly whims. As more mature Christians, we may need encouragement to maintain and hold steadfast to those behavioral changes.

One of the most common criticisms I hear from skeptics of our faith is the hypocrisy they see among Christians. That makes me realize that we do the naysayers a huge disservice if we attempt to present ourselves as if we have it all together. In truth, I need Christ because I *don't* have it all together!

When we are stuck in a pattern of codependency, we might unwittingly act out a script instead of keeping the conversation honest and authentic. I am a Christ follower, and if I am straight about that it is clear that I am no better or worse than my fellow man or woman. My faith means I need to hold on, especially in times of temptation, to the One who lives in me for strength. No pretending is necessary to glorify God.

I hold on to His Spirit as my guide, rather than performing with good words or behavior that may be as fleeting as the wind.

Practice for Healing and Strength

A STRONGHOLD ON BOUNDARIES (page 148): This week take a deeper look at how you carry yourself in mainstream culture. Do you stand firm in your boundaries as a way to glorify God, or do you pretend?

Dear Heavenly Father,

Inspire me to be true with myself and in my relationships, holding to the boundaries of honest conversation and loving deeds. I pray that others will see You through my flawed humanness. Despite my flaws, I commit to a firm stance, allowing You to shine through me.

In Jesus' name. Amen.

HOLDING ON TO GOD, YOUR ROCK

He alone is my rock and my salvation, my
stronghold; I will not be greatly shaken.

PSALM 62:2

The songs David wrote inspire me toward God as the one true and solid
presence in life. When I am in the throes of a codependent dance with
someone, I don't always feel I'm on solid and secure ground. I become
angsty, easily frustrated, and just plain miserable because I focus too
much on what others think or feel about me. I tend to ruminate over
something I said or what I could say now to win back that person's good
graces. Instead, I need only to put the brakes on my runaway thoughts
long enough to remember I can choose to stand on the rock of salvation.

The world will not come crashing down when I let go of what binds
me to codependence. On the contrary, when I give my troubles to God, I
am less shaken as I acknowledge that He loves me in spite of my human
fallibility. When I'm not so physically rattled, I can then think a situation
through with God's clarity. I can focus not so much on what is behind me
but more on what I might like to change in the future or repair presently.
Ultimately, I release my anxiety about how others perceive me by allowing God to have a stronghold on me as His beloved.

I think about the time I was rushing home from work to watch a
game with my daughter, who was a teenager at the time. I was halfway
home when she called to tell me she wanted to watch the game at her
friend's house instead. I immediately had that deflated feeling in my gut
and something even more upsetting—a sense that she didn't want me
anymore.

I knew I was being shaken and sifted, because this seemed like a big reaction on my part to a small request from my daughter. I got off the phone—probably with a very clipped "yes" since I wanted to say "no" to her very reasonable request—and immediately grabbed for God. My rock and my salvation, He is the One who always welcomes me. In reaching to Him, I recognized the wound that was triggered in me in that moment—a wound from the past of feeling unwanted. Yet this was the common pang of a mother watching her teen find autonomy and I could surrender that to God for His healing touch.

Practice for Strength and Healing

RELYING ON GOD AS YOUR ROCK (page 150): Practice embodying scripture-based truths to feel more solid and clear, moving forward without all of the false messages that create codependency.

Dear Heavenly Father,

You are my rock! You bring me strength and set me on solid ground whenever I veer into unstable territory, every time. Thank You for helping me return again and again to the security of Your love and salvation. Ultimately, what You think of me is all that matters—and I rest in confidence that You love me unconditionally!

In Jesus' name. Amen.

FOCUS FIRST ON HOME AND FAMILY

But if anyone does not provide for his own, and especially for those of his household, he has denied the faith and is worse than an unbeliever.

1 TIMOTHY 5:8

Paul is pretty clear on what God desires of us in our walk with Him. All the efforts we make outside of our household have little impact if we are not engaged and giving first to our own domains. It can be easy to get sucked into all the things behind the scenes that have us paying more attention to our work or social media than showing interest in our children or partner—and yet, on the surface, we might look like the perfect family.

In codependency, we can be tempted to try and get others to like us so that we feel valuable and lovable. Yet we are eternally valued and loved—despite others' feelings about us. No matter who you are, what has happened to you, or what you have done, God could not love you any more than He does right now! He wants you to wholeheartedly embrace this truth in all your circumstances. So, maybe today, while you bask in God's love, turn away from the social media distractions or excessive work demands to focus on your family and others God entrusted you with in relationship. When we prioritize our loved ones, we become aware that we are divinely known and genuinely valued.

Practice for Strength and Healing

THE POWER OF INFLUENCE (page 128): Consider how you might better care for those in your household by aligning with God's will for them.

Dear Heavenly Father,

Moments with my loved ones matter more than all the social media "likes" in this world. Help me, Lord, to provide for the practical and emotional needs of my household today. Hedge me in when my mind wants to escape to superficial distractions.

In Jesus' name. Amen.

SEPARATE BUT NEVER ALONE

But all deserted me; may it not be counted
against them. But the Lord stood with me and
strengthened me, so that through me the
proclamation might be fully accomplished.

2 TIMOTHY 4:16–17

In Paul's letter to Timothy, he recounts all the disciples who have left him. The picture he paints of being deserted to walk this journey alone hits home for many. The disappointment and hurt of being let down by those we love can be jarring. The sense of isolation and even fear when being on our own can feel overwhelming.

Yet Paul gives hope that we can journey alone at times. Not only will we join up again with others, but in the meantime, the Lord stands with us and strengthens us. I believe God even intends this at times, especially if He feels we are leaning too heavily on our companions. God wants to give us strength through His presence in our lives, knowing that others will not always be along with us for every leg of the journey.

If you are usually part of the crowd, maybe God wants you to stand apart so His light can shine through you specifically. Paul is honest about his feelings of desertion, and he quickly references that this not be counted against his sojourners. Rather, he recognizes the Lord is with him. God will even strengthen him to achieve the accomplishment set before him. It is good to be in community, but when we are flying solo, we are only separate but *never alone.*

Practice for Healing and Strength

RELYING ON GOD AS YOUR ROCK (page 150): Of course you enjoy fellowship as part of a community. Yet at times, only God sustains you—learn to savor your alone time with Him.

Dear Heavenly Father,

I acknowledge that even in solitude I am never alone. You are a God so faithful that even when I feel deserted and lonely, You are with me. May I feel Your holy presence today and all the days of my life.

In Jesus' name. Amen.

BETRAYED BY THE ONES YOU LOVE

For my father and my mother have forsaken
me, but the Lord will take me up.

PSALM 27:10

Have you ever felt betrayed by those closest to you? Although it may have been a friend, a spouse, or an adult child who betrayed you, I specifically chose this scripture because David laments that those we most trust seem able to inflict the most hurt.

Notice how David illustrates a universal truth that humans, even those close to us, can disappoint and hurt us, merely based on the fact that they are imperfect. In our culture, we are quick to label. I cringe every time I hear someone adamantly label another person as "safe" or "unsafe," or "toxic." The truth is that we are all potentially safe and unsafe in our capacity to harm one another (not to mention ourselves).

I would like to say that my friends most often feel safe with me, in that I offer a nonjudgmental space to talk things through, and yet this is not always true. When I am being especially hard on myself and most critical, I might let that spill over into my interactions with others, and in those times, I am not the safest source of nonjudgmental input. We *all* have human tendencies to judge and betray.

Fear of betrayal doesn't give us permission to wall ourselves off and never trust anyone again. Actually, quite the opposite is true—turn to faith when in fear and for the protection of boundaries, if needed. I believe David is lamenting that betrayal and hurt is just the truth of our experiences as humans, and yet he rightfully praises God for giving us a safe space for retreat. He is reliable and consistent in His offering of relief during and after the storm. The Lord is *always* readily available to lift you up! He is the perfect parent who wholly and persistently has our best interests at heart. Human betrayal is tolerable held up against the light of His trustworthy faithfulness.

Practice for Strength and Healing

EMPOWERMENT, COURTESY OF GOD (page 144): Take a good look at those you have walled yourselves off from because they have hurt you. Journaling your hurts and being honest with your pain is a prelude to leaning into God as your perfect parent to help you heal from past betrayals.

> *Dear Heavenly Father,*
>
> *You are the perfect parent. You are always present for me to fall back on when I feel betrayed by someone I trusted. I need You to lift me up, comfort me, and stand me upright again so I can move forward in relationship. Thank You for understanding my hurt and seeing me through the process of healing.*
>
> *In Jesus' name. Amen.*

THE ARMOR OF GOD

In addition to all, taking up the shield of faith
with which you will be able to extinguish
all the flaming arrows of the evil one.

EPHESIANS 6:16

Throughout Ephesians, Paul speaks of being in relationship with one another as Christ followers. He ends his letter by imploring seekers to wear the armor of God, as he knows we can be vulnerable in relationships most of all. The shield referenced in the above verse is helpful in visualizing how some boundaries work.

Imagine a shield Paul might use during his time in AD 62. It would be made of sturdy steel and large enough to cover much of his body. Shields were used to not only personally protect from active attack but also to set up a barrier to close a line of attack. Setting boundaries has been criticized as an un-Christian act, and yet Paul encourages us to take up our shield, our spiritual protection.

Taking up the shield of faith can look like an emotional boundary by which we envision God keeping us secure in His territory, even in the midst of turmoil around us. Or we can imagine holding up the shield to protect our body, heart, or mind from a personal attack. Often, I encourage imagining a tangible object, such as a bubble or window screen, to act as a shield to help tolerate necessary yet painful communications with a loved one. Visualizing something tangible reminds us of how God can shield us when we trust in Him, helps soften the sting, and allows us to hear vital information that will help us grow our relationships.

Practice for Strength and Healing

MODERATION IN MATTERS OF THE HEART (page 152): Imagine the shield of faith that will keep your heart protected. Stay heart-centered through contemplative prayer.

Dear Heavenly Father,

I love Your visual examples, Your Word in the Bible, of how to experience Your protection. You know how practical humans can be. You meet me where I am, and I'm grateful for that. You are my shield, my protector.

In Jesus' name. Amen.

TAKING A GOOD LOOK WITHIN

Behold, You desire truth in the innermost being,
and in secret You will make wisdom known to me.

PSALM 51:6

As David pleads for God to forgive him his sins of adultery and murder, I imagine he is imploring God to make him a man of integrity—a man strong enough to seek self-awareness and understand his innermost motives. David knows God can transform him to know and seek true wisdom.

I think most of us can relate to David's repentance. At least once in our lives, perhaps we committed a sin and then only *after* the offending act, we question ourselves: *Why would I ever have done that?* Identifying our motivations is key to understanding our behavior. Uncovering such motivations requires a very intentional look to that "innermost being" David references. Only then can we become wise to what unmet need or desire we are trying to fulfill. Once we uncover those, we have greater control over *if* or *how* we might meet them.

Take, for example, Greg, who has been in a relationship with a married woman for years. Greg felt abandoned by his mother as a young adolescent boy, after she left him to start a new family. Greg recognized he was replaying the same scenario in his adult life, wanting a woman who was largely unavailable. Once Greg gained clarity by tapping into his innermost being, he could choose and act with greater integrity and wisdom. He committed to spending more time with God, experiencing the reparative feelings of being chosen by his Father rather than looking to a relationship that was destructive to so many people on so many levels.

Practice for Strength and Healing

FINE-TUNING YOUR EXPECTATIONS (page 136): This week you will take time to explore your innermost being, allowing God to speak wisdom to you about what He can provide.

Dear Heavenly Father,

You make it possible for me to explore the hidden parts of me without fear. You will show me the way and grant me the courage to live in greater freedom, wisdom, and truth. Thank You for walking this journey with me. You never leave me or forsake me.

In Jesus' name. Amen.

HAPPY WIFE, HAPPY LIFE?

When a man takes a new wife, he is not to go
out with the army, nor be assigned any duty;
he shall be free at home for one year and shall
make his wife whom he has taken happy.

DEUTERONOMY 24:5

I have to shoot straight with you: as a therapist who has worked to help make marriages successful for the last twenty-plus years, I think we have widely misunderstood this and other scriptures to mean "happy wife, happy life." Even though I have heard this phrase various times at church functions, I would actually call this out as one of the main slogans of the codependency dynamic.

I conceptualize that this Old Testament instruction from God applies more appropriately to the allowance for husbands to be available and responsive to their brides in the early days of building a secure marital bond. I don't believe this means that it is anyone's job to *make* their spouse happy. That's an impossible feat! I drive this point home throughout the book—we *cannot* control another person's feelings. We can, however, control our motives and behaviors in relationship. We can even influence one another with true Christian love.

God has demonstrated throughout history how readily available He is to respond to the cries of His people (Deuteronomy 4:7). This is the way of His covenant marriage to all. He shows us repeatedly and consistently what true Christian love requires: attentiveness, availability, responsiveness, faithfulness, freedom, unity, and so much more. In doing our best to provide the same to our loved ones, we build healthy God-centered relationship bonds.

In contrast, when we appease a partner just to get what we believe will be "a happy life," we aren't acting on the truth that God calls us to in relationship.

Practice for Strength and Healing

LETTING GOD TAKE INVENTORY (page 142): You will examine what you really pour into your relationships versus seeking to appease a partner to get what you want. This can be a hard inventory to take, but trust that God has your best life in store!

Dear Heavenly Father,

Your love is perfect. I want to learn to love well. Guide me to release the temptation to control other people's feelings and to positively influence them with the love You flow through me.

In Jesus' name. Amen.

BEING RESPONSIBLE TO GOD, NOT FOR GOD

Stop striving and know that I am God.

PSALM 46:10A

Many have probably heard this verse a thousand times or more in its multiple iterations about connecting in stillness with God's good grace. This is God's invitation, which He makes many times throughout the Bible, for us to accept His power and guidance.

Think of it this way: God wants us to be responsible to Him by recognizing our role in aligning with His will. As His children, we have a responsibility *to* listen and obey Him; as His friend, a responsibility *to* walk with Him; as His witnesses, *to* talk about Him; as His bride, *to* love Him. He doesn't ask us, ever, to be responsible *for* Him. God is . . . God. He needs help from no one to be who He is.

When we errantly move into a sense of being responsible for God, we perform out of our own strength. We start apologizing for everything and/or we focus on controlling the outcome, ultimately crashing and burning due to our limited and misguided energies.

God asks us to abide in His holiness, strength, power, light, and love so He can flow through us. It's the idea of being an open and willing vessel—we can earnestly seek and trust that God shines His purpose through us according to His will, which is perfectly fitted to our needs. When I wait on the Lord's cues and allow Him to work through me, my burden is truly lighter and my rest plentiful (Matthew 11:28–30).

Practice for Strength and Healing

BEING RESPONSIBLE "TO" VERSUS "FOR" (page 154): This week you will practice the posture, internally and externally, of allowing God to be God—and giving yourself rest in this truth.

Dear Heavenly Father,

You are more powerful than I ever could be. I am so thankful You do not require me to work harder for You but rather to surrender to You—what a relief. Father, have Your way in me, for You are God and I am a willing vessel.

In Jesus' name. Amen.

COMPASSION OVER SACRIFICE

Now go and learn what this means: "I desire compassion, rather than sacrifice," for I did not come to call the righteous, but sinners.

MATTHEW 9:13

Jesus quotes the Old Testament, the language of the Pharisees, to propel them to true Christian love. "I desire loyalty rather than sacrifice," as is written in Hosea 6:6. Jesus makes clear that He came to fulfill, not abolish, the Law (Matthew 5:17), so His reference to the book of Hosea indicates that He wants us to go beyond the ritual sacrifice to the heart of the matter.

Jesus is always showing us how to love God and others to the depths of our soul, not just as an act or for outward appearances. Anyone can claim an act of sacrifice ("I gave up my career for you," for example), but if that so-called sacrifice is not fueled by compassion for the other person, it is for naught, or perhaps is even a show of perceived martyrdom. I think about how we obligate ourselves at times to make sacrifices of time, money, and energy, but Christ is asking us to give compassion, have mercy, and express love. Choosing compassion brings us to a greater connection with God than any call to sacrifice ever could.

Let's not forget that the depth of connection Jesus calls us to requires humility for us to receive His offering. We can rarely give out to others when we do not allow ourselves to first experience God. Next time you feel unjustly sacrificed, search instead for the sense of compassion God has placed in you.

Practice for Strength and Compassion

ALIGNING WITH JESUS (page 156): This week you will pray for God to build your compassion and connection to others. Who provides the best example of that? Jesus can be our model.

> *Dear Heavenly Father,*
>
> *You brought a living example of the depth of Your love, in Jesus Christ. You stretch me beyond my outward behavior to an infinite depth of genuine love and care. May You help me to connect with compassion for those You place in my experience today.*
>
> *In Jesus' name. Amen.*

FEAR IS NOT YOUR FRIEND . . . NOR ENEMY

Do not fear, for I am with you; do not be
afraid, for I am your God. I will strengthen
you, I will also help you, I will also uphold
you with My righteous right hand.

ISAIAH 41:10

Fear has its purpose. After counseling many individuals who have lived through horrific circumstances, I am convinced God created the emotion of fear within us for the adrenaline spike we need for a fight, flight, or freeze response when real danger is in our path. Sadly, fearful moments can imprint so strongly on the brain that some people continue to live in fear long after the immediate danger is gone. Lingering fears can bring a dark feeling of isolation and being alone that a secure bond with our Heavenly Parent can cure.

My husband and I hosted some dear friends and their four-year-old daughter, and watching this little girl run so freely around our big grassy backyard captivated me. I was even more entranced when the evening grew dark. The girl's mom and I sat talking on the back patio with one small corner light to brighten up some of the yard where she was playing. Yet I noticed with astonishment as she ran to the darkest corner of the yard and showed no fear. On the contrary, she was so gleeful that she jumped and laughed and showed off how far she could run. It brings me to tears thinking of this, because she was so secure in the presence of her loving mom that the dark had no fearful effects on her. That's how I want to feel about my Heavenly Parent—knowing He is nearby, even in my darkest hours.

Sometimes when I am isolated and alone, I admit, I fear. Yet I am thankful when I recall that my Heavenly Father is always right here with me. My body, heart, and mind can relax into His loving care.

Practice for Strength and Healing

ALLOWING SCRIPTURE TO BE PERSONAL AND POWERFUL (page 157): This week you will feel into biblical verses as a visceral experience, so that you not only know but also feel how God can relax your brain and body to swap out fear for His presence.

Dear Heavenly Father,

I want to run freely and even venture into uncharted or unfamiliar territory, trusting You are with me. When I feel the sting of fear holding me back, let my body relax into Your strong but gentle embrace and ever-present support.

In Jesus' name. Amen.

WEEK 25

PRAY . . . EVEN FOR
THE SMALL STUFF

Until now you have asked for nothing
in My name; ask and you will receive,
so that your joy may be made full.

JOHN 16:24

Whether it's to escape the lion's den, like Daniel; to be untouched by the flames like Shadrach, Meshach, and Abed-nego; or to call off and then down the rain as Elijah did, the Bible shows us example after example of how prayer never ceases to bring us more amazement of God's glory.

But what about those small prayers, for matters that seem relatively unimportant in the grand scheme? Well, those seemingly insignificant moments matter to God just as much as do tragedy and disaster. Make no mistake, God cares about every hair on your head (Luke 12:7) as well as what's rolling around inside it!

While I have sought professional help for my unhealthy relationship with false idols, such as food, I have learned to lean into the power of prayer and seek God's will in the midst of my humanity. I confess that, early on, I maybe prayed He would allow me to bypass the natural consequences of my extra body weight, with little effort on my end to change unhealthy eating habits.

As I've matured with God, I recognize my need to regularly pray that He conform me to His will. So, I sometimes pray for eight seconds at a time—just a quick prayer: "God, help me resist temptation," or, "Lord, show me what I am truly needing or desiring." I say a simple eight-second prayer to God as I stand in my kitchen or while taking a walk, repeating it over and over until the temptation passes. It's not about timing the prayer, but rather pausing to say a short prayer of surrender. Reciting a brief prayer or scripture verse can refocus my attention on God and what I am truly needing and not on the unsatisfactory temporary fix.

Practice for Strength and Healing

LETTING GO AND LETTING GOD (page 158): This week you will learn to ask and consider what He would want you to receive to wholly fill you with joy.

Dear Heavenly Father,

You are always accessible to me in prayer. I don't know how I would survive without You! I appreciate that there is no wrong way to pray when I am earnestly seeking You. No prayer is too big or too small for Your greatness.

In Jesus' name. Amen.

HE GIVES YOU
FREE WILL TO CHOOSE

It was for freedom that Christ set us free;
therefore keep standing firm and do not
be subject again to a yoke of slavery.

GALATIANS 5:1

I often think about how God could have auto-programmed us to obey Him—essentially, to be robots—but instead He gives us free will to choose or not choose Him. Allowing us the autonomy to choose Him is true unconditional love.

Let's look at this from the codependent stance, where we often feel like we "have to" meet certain expectations. We somehow enslave ourselves into obligation, which leads to resentment or avoidance. While working with many Christians who strive to follow God, I often hear, "I have to, to be a good Christian."

Imagine if your spouse were to say to you, "Yes, I will have sex with you because I have to." This doesn't seem very appealing, now, does it?

Jesus invites us to choose so we can fully engage in the freedom of that choice. In our free will, we can actually love the fiercest. Moving our internal question—*Do I choose to?* or even *Do I want to?*—moves us closer to the heart shift Jesus is really asking for.

I think about the potter and the vessel metaphor again, recognizing that if I am not filled up by the Lord, I have very little to pour out. If I obligate myself to pour out regardless, I am likely to do so with a spirit of resentment or frustration. This is not because I'm a bad Christian but because a sense of obligation actually defies the joy of living in the freedom of choice.

Practice for Strength and Healing

BASKING IN THE FREEDOM OF GOD (page 127): This week you live fully in the freedom Christ gives you and consider your internal words, which have the potential to move you back into bondage.

Dear Heavenly Father,

There are none like You, Lord. Thank You for granting me the freedom to choose. By that freedom alone, I can breathe. I choose to love You and to love others well. Fill me and empower me with Your amazing love, I pray.

In Jesus' name. Amen.

ALLOWING GOD TO SEARCH YOUR HEART

Search me, God, and know my heart; put me
to the test and know my anxious thoughts;
and see if there is any hurtful way in me,
and lead me in the everlasting way.

PSALM 139:23–24

My Bible practically falls open to this psalm whenever I set it down,
as I have come back to it hundreds of times, usually while in relational
turmoil, to let Him show me what may be my responsibility to repair.
David, a strong and humble man who is after God's heart, shows us the
importance of letting God take our inventory and lead us back to the
everlasting way.

Emotions are just a signal that something may need attention in our
innermost being. Therefore, whenever I feel unsettled, especially in relationship, I invite God into this place with me. I think specifically of a time
when I was troubled with a colleague and was certain my feelings were
signaling an important lesson for me to consider. I wanted God to read
my heart and help me see a solution for what was troubling me. I appreciate how David models for us his bold surrender to God: "Put me to the
test," he says. He is inviting God to examine what he may have done or
experienced to bring on his anxiety—and then, most important, asks God
to lead him from the emotional mire and redirect him to a better way.
Don't be shy about letting God in. David rejoices that we can trust God to
think positively toward us (Psalm 139:17).

With this in mind, I knew I could trust God to help me see my part in the trouble with my colleague. Upon sitting quietly and prayerfully, open to God's voice, I recognized that I hadn't been clear with this colleague, and I was acting out passive-aggressively. I took a healthy risk going back to this colleague to repair the damage even if she didn't respond positively. God led me to act with integrity—the way everlasting.

Ask this good and merciful God to show you if there is "any hurtful way" in you. Remember He is gentle and will give plentifully in His loving-kindness. My prayer toward interdependence is that He help me honor who He made me to be as I navigate the relationships of my life. I can do this only when I take responsibility for my part in unhealthy patterns and seek the Lord to gently guide me into steps of reconnection with self and others.

Practice for Strength and Healing

KNOWING YOU ARE ENOUGH (page 124): Sit with God, allowing Him to examine your innermost being, to show you where you may be straying from His everlasting way. Humble yourself to depend on Him to lead you back on track.

Dear Heavenly Father,

You are so gentle and kind in spirit. Thank You for bringing me to an honest place within, where I can lean on You as my merciful guide who points me back to the way everlasting. Help me walk in Your way, I pray.

In Jesus' name. Amen.

YOU MAY PRAY, BUT IT'S GOD WHO SAVES

He rescues, saves, and performs signs and miracles in heaven and on earth, He who has also rescued Daniel from the power of the lions.

DANIEL 6:27

The New Testament brings with it the good news of our Savior. And yet, long before the blessings of Christ, time and time again in the Old Testament, we see the saving grace of God. The rescue of Daniel from the lions' den is just one example.

As much as we may love and, therefore, fear for our children, friends, and family members when they seem to be walking into a lion's den, it's key to remember that rescue and salvation are not in our power to give. In fact, sometimes our loved ones need to walk through difficulties to get to the point where they might be open to hearing God's loving and gentle call.

This is one of the hardest requests for some of us to accept—God asking us to release control when we see our loved ones self-destruct. He knows what it will take to call back His child to Him, and sometimes earthly hardships bring about the most clarity for our human minds.

Please don't misunderstand and think this is all or nothing. Staying attuned to the times when God may prompt you to help a loved one is key to living interdependently. Listen for the Lord's prompting on when and how you offer healthy support. Helping your loved one seek health is different from feeling responsible to save or rescue them. Until they ask for support toward a healthier path, allow space for God to speak to them. Bearing one's burden is more about sojourning together, versus taking over responsibility or rescuing one from the burdens God has allowed. Discern when to back off and let Him do the rescuing. Releasing yourself from this responsibility can feel difficult at times, but in exchange, you are given a much-needed spirit of peace.

Practice for Strength and Healing

GOD TO THE RESCUE! (page 138): This exercise walks you through the necessary dialogue you may need to have with God so you can give back what rightfully belongs to Him: rescue and salvation.

Dear Heavenly Father,

Thank You for being responsible for all Your children. Inspire me to release the care of my loved ones to You. My heart feels like it is being torn in two to not have control in rescuing friends or family in need. Yet I know You are trustworthy and that my best effort toward saving someone is to let You.

In Jesus' name. Amen.

THE PERILS OF EXPECTING WITHOUT ASKING

Now as they were traveling along, He entered a village; and a woman named Martha welcomed Him into her home. And she had a sister called Mary, who was also seated at the Lord's feet, and was listening to His word. But Martha was distracted with all her preparations; and she came up to Him and said, "Lord, do You not care that my sister has left me to do all the serving by myself? Then tell her to help me." But the Lord answered and said to her, "Martha, Martha, you are worried and distracted by many things; but only one thing is necessary, for Mary has chosen the good part, which shall not be taken away from her."

LUKE 10:38–42

There are so many important lessons to glean from the passage above. The most glaring perhaps is how we can often get distracted with what we feel we need *to do* for the Lord, without even taking the time to sit at His feet and hear from Him first. However, let's look at the more subtle message about relationships—and how Jesus mediates the relationship dynamics between Martha and Mary.

Martha assumes a responsibility for Mary, but it's possible it was not directly communicated that Mary is expected to cohost the guest. Worse yet, Martha even tries to pull a power play on Jesus in persuading Him to get Mary to do the serving.

Maybe you can relate to volunteering your child or spouse to take part in an activity with you when you haven't even given them the option to decide for themselves. And when they don't follow through—or do so begrudgingly—maybe you then want to push them to meet your expectation.

Codependent tendencies can lead us to expect and assume responsibility on another person's behalf. This only means we have crossed a line—we are trying to control another. Martha is a gracious host to invite Jesus into her home, and He offers a fine demonstration that He doesn't try to control us. He allows us free will to choose "the good part" or the distraction, without shame.

Practice for Strength and Healing

FINE-TUNING YOUR EXPECTATIONS (page 136): Consider surrendering yourself to Jesus' feet, and listen—hear what He is calling *you* to, not others.

Dear Heavenly Father,

I know I can be a busybody, trying to do all kinds of actions for You instead of just sitting and soaking in the words You have for me this day. Please help me to sit at Your feet and to surrender to what You want me to hear today.

In Jesus' name. Amen.

ATTUNING TO OTHERS, WITHOUT LOSING YOURSELF

Jesus, again being deeply moved within, came to the tomb. Now it was a cave, and a stone was lying against it. Jesus said, "Remove the stone." Martha, the sister of the deceased, said to Him, "Lord, by this time there will be a stench, for he has been dead four days." Jesus said to her, "Did I not say to you that if you believe, you will see the glory of God?"

JOHN 11:38–40

Four days—that's how long Jesus' friend Lazarus has been dead before He arrives at his tomb. "Lazarus, come out!" He hollers after the tombstone is removed from the cave's opening. And out walks Lazarus, alive and well!

In the story of Lazarus' death and resurrection, we see very clearly this idea that Jesus intends for us to be the kind of people who can be lovingly influenced. Jesus is moved by the grief of Mary and Martha, sisters to Lazarus. Jesus does not get offended when they cry upon His arrival, "Lord, if You had been here, our brother would not have died." He instead uses his innate ability to be deeply attuned with them through empathy and "Jesus wept"; while remaining steadfast in His truth, which is key to successful interdependence.

This cycle of allowing ourselves to be lovingly influenced and attuned to others is critical to being supportive of one another emotionally. Jesus knows he has the power to resurrect Lazarus and easily could have charged in reassuring them of His power and control over the situation. Rather, Jesus came in with kindness and heart-to-heart connection, respecting His friends' emotions.

Practice for Strength and Healing

ALIGNING WITH JESUS (page 156): Consider those in your community who may need you to attune to them and whatever they are experiencing. You will invite Jesus to give you a heart like His.

Dear Heavenly Father,

Lord, when my heart breaks, help me turn to the security of Your love and the knowledge that You are in control. I hope to feel secure enough in Your ultimate plan that I can enter into an empathetic connection with those I love.

In Jesus' name. Amen.

SEEKING A BOUNDARY TO HOLD ON TO

Create in me a clean heart, God, and
renew a steadfast spirit within me.

PSALM 51:10

I appreciate the knowledge David expresses in this scripture. He knows he needs God to clean up his heart, trusting God can give him a fresh housecleaning when it comes to his desires, motives, and behaviors. On many occasions, I have asked God to clean up my heart—to bring me back to Him. And yet, what I am probably drawn to most in this passage is that David asks God to create a boundary in him—a boundary that helps him *hold* on to this cleaned-up heart. Without that, I may make a mess of just about any ordeal in a matter of hours.

David is asking God to bring him anew to a sturdy spirit filled with faith that is firm, that has clarity of thought, that is unshakable to the temptations of the world. This is testimony to a particular type of boundary, one of knowing where we stand, of holding fast to what we know to be true in the Spirit and not letting that be muddied by the dynamics of codependency.

Anytime I run across the word "steadfast" in the Bible, it inspires a visceral response of luring me back into this solidness, this clear form that holds faith. That is what a personal boundary feels like to me. When we consistently connect with this felt sense of the steadfast Spirit, it can bring greater peace in the moment, for sure, and ultimately, persistent joy.

Practice for Strength and Healing

A STRONGHOLD ON BOUNDARIES (page 148): This week you will pray fervently for God to clean house in your heart. A cleaned-up heart has better clarity for setting boundaries.

Dear Heavenly Father,

You are a God who will get in the mess with me. You desire to go deep into my heart, where I hold the motives, desires, and feelings behind my behavior and choices. You care more about that deep cleaning than just what I look like from the outside. Lord, help me hold on to the Spirit You give me—it is loving, pure, and good.

In Jesus' name. Amen.

IN ORDER TO CARE FOR OTHERS, YOU NEED HIS CARE IN YOU

And in the early morning, while it was still dark,
Jesus got up, left the house, and went away to
a secluded place, and prayed there for a time.

MARK 1:35

Jesus models our need for God's replenishment. Receiving soul-care from God is vital to being able to extend care to others. Even Jesus shows that only upon receiving this can we then pour it out.

I think of self-care in a deeper way than do many in our current culture. Current culture says I am caring for myself—or even self-indulgent—if I go for a massage or pedicure. I am not negating these activities, which may be nourishing, but consider whether or not they nourish your soul. *Am I feeding my soul what it needs to stay attuned to God and His presence? Am I bringing my emotional and spiritual needs before God? Am I resting enough and eating well? Am I talking to God, and then pausing long enough to listen?* His Spirit lives in us, and therefore we need to direct our focus and awareness within, to our inner being, to fully experience His nourishing soul-care. This is not to say that we should not allow our soul to be fed by those whom God wants to speak through, such as our pastors, our friends, or our wise counsels.

It really is critical that we pour out from a place of having something to give. If my emotional landscape is dry and desolate, my offerings might be clouded by what I need and I won't be able to see what the other is needing. When we feel well cared for, we care well for others.

Practice for Strength and Healing

REPLENISHMENT THROUGH SOUL-CARE (page 160): You will pray for God to show you how to care for your mind, body, and soul, and relationships.

Dear Heavenly Father,

I want to love others well. Please inspire me to care for my body and soul in a way that makes me a sturdy and loving vessel to pour out Your love. I trust You will continue to sustain me in relationships, as I allow You to cherish and nourish me. I surrender to You, O Lord.

In Jesus' name. Amen.

BEING RESPONSIBLE TO, NOT FOR, OTHER ADULTS

Behold, all souls are Mine; the soul of the
father as well as the soul of the son is Mine.

EZEKIEL 18:4

The prophet Ezekiel passes along vital revelation of the new covenant. He gives us a picture of how the Lord God is the sole possessor of every soul and that He will deal justly with *each individual.*

Previously we focused on being responsible *to* God, not *for* God, and this same principle applies to able-bodied adult-to-adult relationships. We have responsibilities *to* each other for the role we play in each other's lives (friend, spouse, coworker, boss, parent), but we will make a mess of things if we try to be responsible *for* others. That is God's job! When we feel responsible for other people, we tend to want to control them and their lives. We might try to get them to behave a certain way, without considering that God has a greater plan to bring them to Him. We are not privy to the bigger picture, which God has in His full view, so faith means trusting Him to be responsible for your loved ones—even if the road they're following appears rocky.

I meet with many parents who feel distraught and powerless over the path their adult child has taken in life. Although I support efforts to help their adult child, in their desperation, some such parents unintentionally enable and attempt to be their child's savior by protecting them from natural consequences. Others deal with the struggle by separating themselves from their child's decisions and therefore disconnect from them completely. Only God can deal justly, so let's trust that our Lord God loves and cares for our children—even in their adulthood—more perfectly than we do. Sometimes, He has to allow His children to get to the end of the road, where they often have nowhere else to go but into His loving embrace.

Practice for Strength and Healing

BEING RESPONSIBLE "TO" VERSUS "FOR" (page 154): You will examine, pray, and practice transferring responsibility for your loved ones to God, who is the loving possessor of each soul.

> *Dear Heavenly Father,*
>
> *Your love is great and so forgiving. I release to You those whom I know I cannot control. Lead me to a mindset of wholly trusting You to care for them. Please prompt my loved ones to swiftly surrender to You when they are traveling tough terrain.*
>
> *In Jesus' name. Amen.*

LET HIS LOVE TRANSFORM YOUR INNER SELF

That He would grant you, according to the riches of His glory, to be strengthened with power through His Spirit in the inner self, so that Christ may dwell in your hearts through faith; and that you, being rooted and grounded in love, may be able to comprehend with all the saints what is the width and length and height and depth, and to know the love of Christ which surpasses knowledge, that you may be filled to all the fullness of God.

EPHESIANS 3:16-19

This string of verses from Ephesians certainly packs a punch, so rich with God's desire for us. Let's break this down.

First, Paul is praying that in all of God's glory, power, and goodness that we be empowered to respond in the Spirit He instills within us—we don't have to earn it; it is our birthright. This brings us to the reality that we are enough, just as we are—so much so that we are "rooted and grounded" enough to comprehend His love's limitlessness. We are divinely gifted with not just a head knowledge of His love but also truly feeling His love to its fullness in every part of our being—"the inner man," as it's phrased in Ephesians. Paul paints a word picture of love's width, length, height, and depth, so no part of me or my past is left out.

So, let's bring this love to *all* the inner parts of us—even the parts we want to hide or are embarrassed by.

Paul knows that in receiving this love we are transformed. It's a transformation that shifts the heart so we allow others to love us *and* spread that love around to others. This transformation leads to the complete fullness of God. Now, we can be so grounded and assured of ourselves in God that we can freely love others and *be* loved by them. Living interdependently brings about the ability to love another without controlling them or being controlled by them. We learn to accept them, choosing to focus on and appreciate their strengths instead of ruminating on or ridiculing them for their weaknesses. We are much more resilient and able to grow deeper connections—at home, with friends, in the workplace—when we are grounded in the greatest love of all.

Practice for Strength and Healing

GETTING INTO HARMONY (page 162): As a means to get centered with God, you will listen to a song and use the lyrics to help you feel the fullness of His love.

Dear Heavenly Father,

The enormity of Your love is breathtaking. It brings me to my knees to know You love every part of me. You want to fill me full of Your love. You promise not to leave any part of me outside of this great love. My heart swells.

In Jesus' name. Amen.

THE HEART IS A TREASURE

Above all else, guard your heart, for
everything you do flows from it.

PROVERBS 4:23 (NIV)

Guarding our hearts is indeed a biblical principle. It recognizes the world we live in as one that is fallen and imperfect; it acknowledges that we are not perfect in our actions and can sin against one another, even those we love. Guarding the heart is about having healthy boundaries. When we are heart-wounded, we are tempted to internalize this hurt or hurl it outward in revenge. Ancient wise counsel says to protect the heart so good can flow from it toward others and inward to ourselves.

My husband and I love to watch the old version of *The Little Drummer Boy* at Christmastime, because the classic TV special shows that Jesus can pierce emotional darkness in a moment and bring warmth, joy, and peace if we allow Him. Being abandoned, abused, or neglected in childhood can cause such a darkness to take root. As children, we are vulnerable to others safeguarding our hearts. When the adults in our lives fall short, we might experience hurt, anger, and fear that lead us to *over-protect* our hearts. We may become too guarded and disallow the good to penetrate and restore our hearts.

Sometimes, it's the other way around—we perhaps *under-protect,* allowing negative influences in and thereby too often feeling emotionally wounded. In some cases, individuals who don't have a healthy guard for their hearts did not experience protection nor were allowed to have boundaries in childhood. We are often taught—and falsely believe—it is somehow our fault if we feel wounded.

"Above all else" is a strong instruction, in the above verse from Proverbs, that invites us to participate in the process of guarding our hearts with discernment. God will help us discern at what level to guard our hearts in any given situation or with a particular person. There will be moments when we will be instructed to stand back and *not* engage with an open heart.

Practice for Strength and Healing

MODERATION IN MATTERS OF THE HEART (page 152): Do you over- or under-protect your heart? This week you will consider that wise counsel may be instructing you to guard your heart—or open it up.

Dear Heavenly Father,

You give me permission to guard my heart when I need protection. I feel cared for when You recognize my heart is valuable and worthy of safeguarding. Please help me discern when I need to guard my heart in my earthly experiences. Allow what flows from it to be pure and glorifying to You.

In Jesus' name. Amen.

HOW DO YOU LET GO AND LET GOD?

The Lord is near. Do not be anxious about anything, but in everything by prayer and pleading with thanksgiving let your requests be made known to God. And the peace of God, which surpasses all comprehension, will guard your hearts and your minds in Christ Jesus.

PHILIPPIANS 4:5B–7

He promises that He is near. He is listening. I often say that one of the worst human conditions is feeling alone, so let's break down this truth.

Consider how God understands our humanity. Regardless of how many times we have heard the unspoken and untrue rule that "Christians are not to be anxious," God already knows we tend to be anxious. Otherwise, He wouldn't speak through Paul to tell us He will take care of it! His ever-present glory wants to give us peace that surpasses all understanding. Whether we come to Him in humility, gratitude, or need, He is present and in the process of fulfilling your request.

When I am uncertain as to why I feel an underlying buzzing of worry, I recall this scripture and pray with a mindset of giving thanks. I have a God who cares to be near me. He wants to give me peace over whatever I am feeling worry over. He does not shame me for worry. He simply says there is no need for it as long as I *let go* of trying to figure it all out and *let Him* work it out, within me.

God has an extraordinary and mysterious way of giving us peace even when it doesn't make any earthly sense. Embrace that truth, and be confident in Him. Our efforts will always fall short. By the mere fact that it does bypass our comprehension, I know it is God in us and not something we could have worked out on our own. What an amazing God who wants to give us such precious gifts when we just let Him!

Practice for Strength and Healing

LETTING GO AND LETTING GOD (page 158): You will pray in gratitude and make humble requests to God. Then you'll journal about how the inner peace within your spirit is affected when you let go and let Him take the reins.

Dear Heavenly Father,

I appreciate Your reminders that You are near! I am not in this alone, and You never intended for me to manage it all on my own. I release my anxieties to You today. I trust You with everything. You are such an amazing God, keeping watch over my heart and mind today and every day.

In Jesus' name. Amen.

KEEP GOING

He gives strength to the weary, and to the
one who lacks might He increases power.

ISAIAH 40:29

The book of Isaiah is one of my favorites, because it is the clearest Old Testament picture of our coming Savior *and* salvation through hope in God. Isaiah cautions people not to worship the wrong things as they grow more and more weary under the heavy burden of their times. He shares the true hope of God and His everlasting power (Isaiah 40:28). He provides hope of rescue for them in the present day but also promises that more help is on the way with the eternal Savior.

We can relate today, with our current struggles of war, politics, oppression, and even fad culture. Whether you have the larger system on your mind or a more personal context of your everyday struggles, God sees all concerns as worthy of His attention (Matthew 6:25-27).

Taking a new relationship approach, like setting boundaries or practicing more vulnerability, can feel tiresome, especially if we experience setbacks or resistance from others. Isaiah continually fills us with hope that God will see us through the roughest of times. Salvation is not just an idea about the future; salvation is today. The Savior lives in us, giving us strength and power to keep on. Isaiah 40:31 promises, "Those who wait for the Lord will gain new strength." When we are feeling weary, we can proceed gracefully with this new dance of loving interdependence, because He promises to give strength. Allow Him to strengthen you as you take the next steps in your earthly relationships.

Come to Him, unashamed that you need Him to reenergize you—this is the soul-care He knows is vital to your well-being. Only by relying on Him do we have next-level strength to effectively thrive through relationship challenges and other issues. Admitting our weakness gives Him the opportunity to make us strong (2 Corinthians 12:10).

Practice for Strength and Healing:

GETTING INTO HARMONY (page 162): You will spend time basking in God's endless love for you, allowing Him to transform you through the soothing effects of music.

> *Dear Heavenly Father,*
>
> *Your divine energy never fails. I am always able to increase my strength by leaning into You as my energy source. Uplift me throughout this day and those to come. I put my hope only in You.*
>
> *In Jesus' name. Amen.*

TREAT OTHERS HOW YOU LIKE TO BE TREATED

In everything, therefore, treat people the
same way you want them to treat you,
for this is the Law and the Prophets.

MATTHEW 7:12

As much as I love Jesus' parables, I also love it when He just shoots us straight between the eyes. No interpretation necessary. He makes it very clear that we are to treat one another in the same ways we want to be treated.

Think about how we intentionally or unintentionally treat each other in the dance of codependency. We may treat another like a pack mule, expecting that person to carry the weight of the relationship, or maybe we have a partner who treats the other as a fragile bird that can't handle the slightest storm. We may even give to others what we don't give to self—a false belief that they are somehow more worthy or valuable to God than we are.

For people involved in the codependency dance, they each have their God-given strengths, talents, and purposes. I see how resourceful and creative God makes us as social beings. Often no specific behavior of codependency is necessarily wrong—it's more about how we overuse a certain action step. Take, for example, Caroline, who wanted to give her friend the benefit of the doubt when she dismissed Caroline's feelings in their friendship. Her friend frequently told her, "You shouldn't feel that way" or simply brushed her off. When Caroline continued to extend grace for this dismissal and not voice to her friend that this was hurtful, Caroline's excessive display of mercy led to a codependent dance. I asked

Caroline to imagine the situation in reverse: Would she want to know if her friend felt Caroline was dismissing *her* emotions? Caroline immediately answered "yes." I encouraged her to consider Matthew 7:12 to inspire the strength and courage to be honest with her friend.

No one is of greater importance than another (Galatians 3:26–29). We are all considered equal in God's eyes. As we are called to treat others with honor, let us not neglect treating God's creation in us with honor as well.

Practice for Strength and Healing

REPLENISHMENT THROUGH SOUL-CARE (page 160): Feeling depleted? This week you will take care of yourself. This week's exercise is a lot of fun if not a little, um, jarring.

> *Dear Heavenly Father,*
>
> *We are divinely created by You—each of us equal in Your eyes. I want to never deface what You have purposed in me, and respect and appreciate others in kind. Direct my focus not on this world and its order of value but on You and Your desire for each of us to be loved and treated with care.*
>
> *In Jesus' name. Amen.*

LOOK FORWARD, NOT BACKWARD

Brothers and sisters, I do not regard myself as having taken hold of it yet; but one thing I do: forgetting what lies behind and reaching forward to what lies ahead, I press on toward the goal.

PHILIPPIANS 3:13–14A

It's refreshing to hear Paul humbly acknowledge that he hasn't perfected the practice of living out of a Christian spirit at all times. He, however, gives hope that we can still look ahead and move toward the "upward call of God in Christ Jesus" (Philippians 3:14). Laying behind our old patterns in relationships and moving toward the greater call of interdependency and true Christian love can be challenging, but, at the end of the day, rewarding.

Although the above scripture is highlighted in my Bible, I hadn't referenced back to it in quite some time until a dear friend, who had a terribly dark year of betrayal, boldly proclaimed her focus on what lies ahead, not what is behind her. I have loved and respected this friend for more than twenty years, and her graceful shift in focus after being betrayed by a colleague is inspiring. She knows she has the capacity to try and manipulate a different outcome or attempt to control the other person's feelings, but instead, she leaned into God. She allowed Him to shift her feelings and guide her response to this colleague.

The situation was unjust, and my friend could have handled it with revenge or by seeking retribution. While she didn't go to those extremes, she knew she too had acted poorly. And then, she allowed God to usher

her to Philippians 3:13, which helped her move toward healthier interactions. Rather than being paralyzed by the past, she took the brave step of being straight and clear with this colleague about how she felt and the harm done to their relationship. This was important for any chance of a future between them, including my friend asking forgiveness for how she had acted in the situation. My friend depended on God to order her steps forward. By processing her hurt and anger in healthy ways, as well as owning her offensive behaviors, she was able to engage more interdependently. I love this friend with my whole heart and cherish how she strives toward living in His Spirit.

Practice for Strength and Healing

GROWING YOUR BLESSINGS (page 164): In this exercise, you will focus your energies on the path forward, allowing God to order your steps toward the call of Christ Jesus.

> *Dear Heavenly Father,*
>
> *Help me release the burdens of my past, which I cannot change. I want to keep my focus forward to what You have in store. I know You are in the business of giving life and abundantly so. May I get a taste of this today.*
>
> *In Jesus' name. Amen.*

INDEED, WE NEED EACH OTHER

Be devoted to one another in brotherly love;
give preference to one another in honor.

ROMANS 12:10

Paul teaches us how to relate to one another in service to God, and although he calls for dependence on our Savior (Romans 11:36), he also reminds us to be devoted to one another. He urges us not to neglect our relationships, and to live out God's plan and purpose for us. When we are devoted to one another, we willfully engage in interdependent relationships that consider the care and needs of all.

When God speaks through the Holy Spirit to the prophets and teachers at Antioch, He sets aside Paul and Barnabas for a work He has called them to (Acts 13:2). I imagine God had an intended purpose for a partnership in which their individual gifts and talents would complement each other to bring many to Christ. As scripture states, they were "being sent out by the Holy Spirit." Being in that type of partnership, the pair needed certain commitments from each other to stay engaged in such a synchronized way. This synchronicity was threatened when Barnabas wanted Mark to travel with them back to where they had already ministered. Paul took a strong stance against this, due to Mark previously "deserting" them and the work, so he and Barnabas went their separate ways (Acts 15). However, this did not paralyze them or hinder them from going forward with their ministries. Although they may have grieved the loss of their unique partnership, they were dependent only on One.

Practice for Strength and Healing

BEING RELIANT, NOT DEPENDENT (page 165): Consider your dependency on God and what would be missing from your life without this connection. Then think about your closest relationships. Do you put more emphasis on your relationship with others . . . or with God?

> *Dear Heavenly Father,*
>
> *Thank You for blessing me with the people in my life—some for longer durations than others, but always for the amount of time You deem necessary. You keep me dependent on You alone, and yet, have been so gracious to give me sojourners along the way. I yearn to experience loving and reliable relationships from this day forward.*
>
> *In Jesus' name. Amen.*

MOTIVE MATTERS

As for you, my son Solomon, know the God of your
father, and serve Him wholeheartedly and with
a willing mind; for the Lord searches all hearts,
and understands every intent of the thoughts.

1 CHRONICLES 28:9A

But wait until the Lord comes, who will both
bring to light the things hidden in the darkness
and disclose the motives of human hearts.

1 CORINTHIANS 4:5B

The above scriptures—one from the Old Testament, the other from the New Testament—show that throughout *all* of history, our motives have always mattered to God. I would venture to say that our motives matter even more than a single codependent behavior. The Lord will bring our motives and intentions into the light. Jesus makes this crystal clear when He reads the thoughts of His doubters and questions them: "Why are you thinking evil in your hearts?" (Matthew 9:4, Mark 2:8, and Luke 5:22).

God *knows* what motivates our actions—nothing goes under the radar. It's noble to consider the impact motive might have on actions and behaviors in codependent scenarios. For example, did you offer to clean your teen son's room as a genuinely helpful gesture—or is it a sneaky excuse to snoop through his stuff?

How might motive change perspective? For example, you might more easily find forgiveness when realizing an offending party had good intentions. The motives from which we behave in interdependency are born of love.

Practice for Strength and Healing

LOVE AS THE MOTIVATOR (page 166): By journaling you will get better acquainted with your inner self and get real about what motivates your actions. Be honest with yourself, bring into the light that which Christ already knows.

> *Dear Heavenly Father,*
>
> *I dare say that my motives and intentions matter more to You than any one action. Thank You for giving me mercy and guiding me to seek the fulfillment of Law, more so than just following the Law.*
>
> *In Jesus' name. Amen.*

DO NOT BE CONSUMED BY ONE ANOTHER

For you were called to freedom, brothers and sisters; only do not turn your freedom into an opportunity for the flesh, but serve one another through love. For the whole Law is fulfilled in one word, in the statement, "You shall love your neighbor as yourself." But if you bite and devour one another, take care that you are not consumed by one another.

GALATIANS 5:13–15

This scripture could take weeks to unpack because it is so full of relational lessons in just three verses. In short, Paul is referencing the freedom of choice we are given to act according to our flesh *or* the Holy Spirit. Pause here for one moment to let this sink in: you get to *choose*. He gives us free will to choose kindness toward one another and ourselves *or* to satisfy our fleeting temptations. I want to drive the idea home that God does not enslave us to laws and rules (shoulds and ought to's) but gives us opportunities to act from personal intention.

Let's also look at the important lesson in Galatians 5:15: if we "bite and devour one another," we run the risk of being "consumed by one another." We may relate to this when we find ourselves venting about a friend or family member because we feel rejected or judged by them. We may be tempted to "bite back" or compare ourselves and get mentally and emotionally "consumed" by what they think about us instead of standing in our holy identity. Part of the destruction of codependent patterns is that we leave our own identity and exchange it for what we think others want of us.

Paul, in Galatians 5, talks to us about how to live in the freedom of interdependence where everyone's identity and needs matter instead of using one another to temporarily satisfy the flesh. Paul warns us to not objectify or use one another as a means to get what we want. Paul cautions both the devourer and the one being devoured, as both will reap the consequences of losing themselves in codependency.

Practice for Strength and Healing

SEEK AND FIND RELATIONSHIP SATISFACTION (page 168): Sit in prayer to ask the Lord to work within your heart so you better choose the good and lasting things over what is temporary and unloving—for yourself and others.

Dear Heavenly Father,

Please help me make good choices. I want to truly take in the love You so readily give and to extend this love to others. When I don't accept what You so graciously give me, I fill it in with temporal fixes that are ultimately unsatisfying and drag me down. Revive me, Lord.

In Jesus' name. Amen.

INTERDEPENDENCE BUILDS CHARACTER AND HOPE

And not only this, but we also celebrate in our tribulations, knowing that tribulation brings about perseverance; and perseverance, proven character; and proven character, hope; and hope does not disappoint, because the love of God has been poured out within our hearts through the Holy Spirit who was given to us.

ROMANS 5:3–5

Although I imagine we are all very familiar with these verses, I want you to notice the plurals—*our* tribulations, *our* hearts. The tribulations we experience from being in relationship with one another actually help us to persevere. Through our interactions, we fuel one another toward personal growth and hope. We can seek hope not only in circumstances or for well-being, but also the one true hope: Jesus Christ and His love.

Think of a turbulent time in your life when you may have drawn inward. Maybe you wanted to be left alone to white-knuckle it or hoped someone would come and just pull you out of the muck. But what about working with others to solve a problem? How often do you consider asking others to move *with* you toward a solution? Not to fix or rescue you, but it helps to have someone to empathize with the anguish and encourage you to keep going. The above scripture celebrates togetherness in tough times.

The growth process might start with sharing honest thoughts, feelings, and relational needs with another. I know many spiritual sojourners who courageously persist in building their character, due to their love of God *and* their friends and family. Hope lives not in unhealthy dependency in these friendships but due to loving fellowship.

Practice for Strength and Healing

GROWING YOUR BLESSINGS (page 164): Consider the plural "we." Who are the sojourners you desire to travel with toward improved character and the ultimate hope?

> *Dear Heavenly Father,*
>
> *Thank You for giving me You! You are my ultimate hope. I praise You for encouraging me to not endure my tribulations alone but to find sojourners who will inspire me toward growth in You. I love You, Lord.*
>
> *In Jesus' name. Amen.*

HOW TO ROLL WITH SELF-CONTROL

But the fruit of the Spirit is love, joy,
peace, patience, kindness, goodness,
faithfulness, gentleness, self-control;
against such things there is no law.

GALATIANS 5:22–23

Pay particular attention to the last of the listed fruit of the Spirit: *self-control*. It's imperative to accept that we are to seek control of ourselves and not anyone else, as tempting as it may be to try and make others do what we want. I often empathize with parents as it can be easier to trust God with our own matters than it is to have faith He will take care of others, especially our adult children. This can take a whole other level of faith for those who have been too other-focused.

Everything outside of my internal being and external expression is truly out of my control. I often counsel people to use "I" statements: "I can control what I say, what I do, where I go, what I allow to continually influence me." God graciously gives me control over much of what I do and think. Yet outside of that, I walk by faith. When I try and control anything outside of myself, I usually end up feeling overburdened, disappointed, or disillusioned.

We are asked to be ambassadors for Christ (2 Corinthians 5:20). That means we represent God through our living, not by dictating how others live. If we don't like the impact someone's behavior has on us, we get to look at what boundaries we can set for ourselves. Boundaries, from a biblical standpoint, are healthy declarations for us to remain safe and secure in Him. Boundaries are not intended to harm or manipulate others. Stay focused on the control God gives us over ourselves.

Practice for Strength and Healing

TO CONTROL . . . OR NOT CONTROL? (page 130): Focus your prayer time this week on what God is asking you to take charge of and what He is asking you to release to Him.

Dear Heavenly Father,

I desire to live by Your loving principles, yet I know I fall short every day. Please help me, Lord, to stay true to my boundaries and what I can control. I release to You my loved ones and their behavior, trusting You are doing a mighty work in them too. I pray for them to surrender to You, and may I do the same.

In Jesus' name. Amen.

GOD-DRIVEN RELATIONSHIP RESTORATION

And the Lord will continually guide you, and satisfy your desire in scorched places, and give strength to your bones . . . and you will be called the repairer of the breach, the restorer of the streets in which to dwell.

ISAIAH 58:11A AND 12B

The idea that God will meet you and satisfy you in the most dry and scorched places can give you exactly the encouragement you need to stay committed to your own healthy engagement within your relationships. In our humanity, we will unintentionally hurt our loved ones, and they us, because we give one another access to our hearts . . . appropriately so, for without access, we would not share reciprocal love. Although we may be tempted to restrict love's access, God shows us that He will strengthen us to love again, repairing and restoring those heart pathways when we let Him.

When we allow God to satisfy our desires or needs, our well-being isn't held captive by a loved one. We then have the strength to take the courageous step of repairing any breach in a broken relationship and restoring *our* actions to healthy ones. Sometimes the repair is a boundary that we need set in order to secure safety for ourself. Other times, a compromise is necessary to finding middle ground. Whatever a relationship might need, seeking God first can help us be strengthened to face the relational repair.

Practices for Strength and Healing

BUT FIRST ... YOUR EMOTIONAL WELLNESS (page 140): Spend time in prayer with God, and then see how He guides you. He is the repairer and restorer of your fractured relationships.

Dear Heavenly Father,

I can come to You with anything. I want to find a way to sustain my relationships when they feel fragile, but I don't always feel strong enough. Lord, help me to feel the satisfaction only You can give to my heart, and give me the courage to seek repair when a relationship feels broken.

In Jesus' name. Amen.

DIVINE STRENGTH TO SET BOUNDARIES

But the Lord is faithful, and He will strengthen
and protect you from the evil one.

2 THESSALONIANS 3:3

I love how Paul seems to reassure us, as much as he is reassuring himself, that we have a God who will protect us. It helps me relate to the fact that Paul felt some sense of worry and even fear as he went into threatening places. Yet he reminded himself, in these moments, of God's faithfulness to *give him* the strength needed for protection.

Boundaries are often misunderstood in codependent relationships. Boundaries are not ultimatums or manipulation tactics. Boundaries are a measure that can protect us and keep us safe emotionally, physically, and sexually. Boundaries come *after* we have made a request to the other person for something we may need for greater security in a relationship. If a loved one does not respond to a request, we still have a Heavenly Father who will provide the security we seek and need. We are not left abandoned, but rather, He promises to give us the strength to set and maintain a boundary. By His faithfulness, we experience His protection.

Working with one particular couple, I noticed the husband often criticized his wife's feelings. He made statements like, "She takes everything so personally," in total disregard for her feelings after he had wielded an insensitive action or word toward her. I saw the wife recoil at times and lash out at others.

I felt she needed protection to stay safe and secure emotionally. She learned to take ownership of her ability to control her emotional safety and say, "I will need to leave the room if you continue to talk to me in this way," and to follow through with just that. She felt strengthened and empowered, knowing she could exit the scenario to keep herself emotionally safe through the faithfulness of her loving and protective Father.

Practice for Strength and Healing

A STRONGHOLD ON BOUNDARIES (page 148): You will practice receiving the strength of your faithful Father, so that you can set boundaries that are helpful for you to be protected.

Dear Heavenly Father,

I pray for the strength to set and maintain healthy boundaries to keep me safe. I love that You require of me only to follow through on the strength You give me, and the protection will follow by Your faithfulness.

In Jesus' name. Amen.

AS LIGHT DISSIPATES DARKNESS

Do not participate in the useless deeds of
darkness, but instead even expose them; for it is
disgraceful even to speak of the things which are
done by them in secret. But all things become
visible when they are exposed by the light,
for everything that becomes visible is light.

EPHESIANS 5:11–13

Bringing our sin or behavior into the light can be one of the most humbling yet fulfilling experiences of our lives. Keeping secrets or lying to
those we love doesn't protect them or us. Many times, I have witnessed
a sense of relief and reunion with a merciful God as others submit to hon-
esty with God, themselves, and others.

I often encourage people to "tell on yourself" as this is a way of
spotlighting what they are thinking or feeling. For example, when a client wants to lose their temper and toss around insults, I counsel them
to instead say something like "I feel like screaming at you right now,
because I don't feel like you are hearing me," or "I want you to hurt like
I'm hurting." This brings to light what they *want* to do without actually
doing it. This is where God can get to work.

When we stow away issues that need attention, we become slaves
to the darkness and act accordingly. So, share your struggles, maybe
even how you feel tempted to sin, and notice that dark and heavy place
within become lighter and less difficult to face. Let God shine His light on
you—no matter what it might expose.

Practice for Strength and Healing

LOVE AS THE MOTIVATOR (page 166): In this practice, you will prayer-fully consider what needs to be brought into the light. Release unfruitful deeds, and allow God to work in your relationships.

Dear Heavenly Father,

Help me accept my humanity and frailty. Sometimes I find myself trying to be above all that, but You graciously remind me that if I can just expose myself to You, Your light will shine through me. Let me be a bearer of Your light, Jesus.

In Jesus' name. Amen.

HEALTHY RELATIONSHIPS INSPIRE SPIRITUAL GROWTH

Looking around at those who were
sitting around Him, He said, "Here are
My mother and My brothers!"

MARK 3:34

Do our relationships encourage greater spiritual growth or hinder it? As Jesus beholds those around Him, those who study and minister alongside Him, He references them as His "mother and brothers," although these are not His actual relatives. His biological mother and brothers are not engaging in spiritual growth with Him at this time. He is referring in Mark 3:34 to His family of God. Jesus is illustrating the intimacy of kinship they share when they grow spiritually and focus on faith-based lessons together.

People do not have to be blood-related or related by marriage or adoption to have familial bonds, as some are considered family by choice. On the flip side, we are not obligated to have codependent relationships with people for the mere fact that they are our biological relatives, so give yourself permission to keep toxic family relationships at arm's length or in small doses.

This idea of focusing on growth of the inner workings of our spiritual being is key to healthy relationships in our lives. This is not to say Jesus' relationships with His biological mother and brothers were unhealthy, but at the time they weren't seeking the same values. If our relationships don't promote spiritual growth within, we may need to reevaluate our kinships.

Practice for Strength and Healing

GROWING YOUR BLESSINGS (page 164): As you sit with scripture, you'll examine the relationships that inspire you to participate with Christ toward your inner growth.

> *Dear Heavenly Father,*
>
> *You have truly blessed me with relationships that don't hinder but instead encourage and inspire my growth in You. I turn to You for discernment when relationships consistently draw me away from You. Help me to set healthy boundaries to stay steadfast in You.*
>
> *In Jesus' name. Amen.*

SACRIFICIAL LOVE

Jesus, knowing that the Father had handed all things over to Him, and that He had come forth from God and was going back to God, got up from supper and laid His outer garments aside; and He took a towel and tied it around Himself.

JOHN 13:3–4

This critical part of the Last Supper gives us one of the most vivid examples of how to love in a truly Christian way. Only through the knowing, intimacy, and surrender Jesus has with the Father is this possible. He knows who He is and what He is entrusted with. Jesus claims His identity, and the feelings of freedom and security it brings, and He can choose what to do with it.

In this claiming of who He is in the Father, He intentionally sheds His rights and sacrifices His garments to take on a position of lower status. A position of true sacrificing means we know what we are sacrificing—we can't sacrifice what we don't have claim to.

We may think making sacrifices makes us *good* Christians, but goodness comes first from knowing and claiming the Father's love. When we sacrifice out of obligation and duty, we bypass the origin of *how* to love. The outpouring of the Father's love propels Jesus to choose that love. Genuine sacrificial love leaves us feeling connected and satisfied, not resentful and spent.

Practice for Strength and Healing

BASKING IN THE FREEDOM OF GOD (page 127): Meditate in the loving embrace of God, and make conscious choices to serve others—because you want to, not because you "should."

Dear Heavenly Father,

Your everlasting love is so overwhelmingly big that I feel there is actually no way for me to hold it all. You propel me to pour it outward. As Jesus made the choice to sacrifice, help me to choose sacrificial love over and over again.

In Jesus' name. Amen.

HE WANTS TO FEED YOUR NEEDS

So if you, despite being evil, know how to
give good gifts to your children, how much
more will your Father who is in heaven give
good things to those who ask Him!

MATTHEW 7:11

I think of how often scripture implores us, "Ask and you shall receive" (Luke 11:9), "Knock and He will answer" (Matthew 7:7). Scripture promises He will offer us the best of all. Christ is not referencing an Amazon package—He is talking about the goodness He gifts to our soul.

In the dance of codependency, we look for the temporary gift—what will help us feel better in this moment. Maybe we look to what another person is doing for us, or perhaps it's about how the other person's mood is affecting us. I may try to fix, rescue, or distance myself from others' negative feelings so *I* feel better.

But God has choreographed a better gift in the dance of interdependency—the fulfillment of being in deep relationship with Him, self, and others. He wants to hear our longings, which psychologist David G. Benner calls "a response of spirit to Spirit," reflecting our spiritual health and appetite, in his book *Sacred Companions: The Gift of Spiritual Friendship Direction*.

God makes us, with physical, emotional, spiritual, and relational needs. He is the source of these needs fulfilled, and sometimes He uses others in our lives to deliver them to fruition.

Practice for Strength and Healing

BUT FIRST . . . YOUR EMOTIONAL WELLNESS (page 140): You will take stock of your potential emotional and spiritual needs, asking God to fill your spirit with His Spirit.

> *Dear Heavenly Father,*
>
> *Thank You for already knowing what my soul needs and for being so willing to meet those needs. I haven't always been taught that my needs and longings are important, so I appreciate Your wanting to give me the best gifts of all. I trust that what You give me is better than what I even think I want or need.*
>
> *In Jesus' name. Amen.*

SHAME SHALL NOT REIGN

Looking only at Jesus, the originator and perfecter
of the faith, who for the joy set before Him
endured the cross, despising the shame, and has
sat down at the right hand of the throne of God.

HEBREWS 12:2

It's unfathomable to really grasp that Jesus took on *all* of our shame, all of our sin, and buried it. Yet without this, I imagine I could barely get out of bed in the morning. When working with fellow sojourners who are having a hard time getting out of the cycle of shame due to repeating patterns of codependency, I remind them that Jesus already gave us an "out."

This "out" starts with "fixing our eyes on Jesus," as allowing our focus to be on Him softens our critical spirit and helps us stay attuned to what He did for us and in us. He detests our shame and wants us to no longer wear those old garments of self-loathing or self-criticism. His joyful intent is that we be set free from that and be clothed in the garments He originally made for us—and will have for us at the end of our journey (Genesis 3:21, Revelations 3:18).

Zechariah 3:4 helps us see that this metaphor of filthy garments refers to our shame. He intends to "remove the filthy garments . . . I have taken your guilt away from you and will clothe you with festive robes." Shame tries to deny who we are as God's good creation, telling us our personhood is bad, ugly, wrong, not enough, and so forth. Shame truly leaves us feeling filthy. However, the healthy guilt we can carry about our behaviors (not our personhood) is not as heavy as this garment of shame, because we have a God who lifts our head and wants to help us turn our actions around, if we allow Him.

When we come to Jesus, "our author and perfecter of faith," He perceives us with love, not with disgust or condemnation. Let's sit with Him until we establish a trust that even in spite of our humanity, He believes in the goodness instilled within us and can help us walk in the way everlasting.

Practice for Strength and Healing

SHOVE OFF, SHAME! (page 146): Focus your eyes on Jesus, allowing Him to tell you who you are and to bury your old filthy garments. You will look at the practical "out" He gives you from shame.

> *Dear Heavenly Father,*
>
> *I lay myself before You, raw and vulnerable to who You say I am. The fact that You know every detail about me and still call me Your beloved makes me weep with relief. You despise all my shame—help me don my new festive robes with dignity, integrity, and most of all, dependence on You.*
>
> *In Jesus' name. Amen.*

THE INTERDEPENDENCE THEME SONG

I can do all things through Him who strengthens me. Nevertheless, you have done well to share with me in my difficulty.

PHILIPPIANS 4:13–14

I smile as I think of this verse as the theme song to interdependence—all right here in two little sentences. Paul knows that his abilities, his strength, and his very life depend on living through the Spirit of Christ Jesus. Yet he makes known the significance of the community of Philippi supporting him through times of affliction, as well.

This is our goal: to know and seek the Lord for all provisions. Without Him, we aren't capable of loving, much less living well. However, we must also recognize the importance of *not* walking through this fallen world in isolation—without support for ourselves and without extending support to others.

Especially, but not exclusively, in our afflictions and weaknesses, we sometimes need others to lean on and provide help—this is beneficial for both giver and receiver. Rather than being independent and isolated from community, recognize that God can provide Himself through other people. Yet sometimes in the codependent dance we are too quick to seek the other person, and God may be wanting to strike a balance. God knows when we need to feel the solidness of how He built us alone and the strength He bestowed within us to hold ourselves up.

A picture that can help us see the balance is that of Moses when the Israelites were battling the Amalekites, and how he was initially able to hold his staff but then after an extended period grew weary of holding it up (Exodus 17:8–12). God enlisted Aaron and Hur to help Moses hold his arms up to the Lord until the battle was won. These companions didn't take Moses' place, but rather all three depended on the Lord together, in community and in support of what Moses was called to do. Without having his brothers to lean on, Moses may have grown too weary to maintain obedience to the Lord. God's plan is for us to sojourn together, to have emotional and relational needs met through one another along the way. He wants us to grow together and trust that the needs we meet for one another are fully dependent on God working through us.

Practice for Strength and Healing

BEING RELIANT, NOT DEPENDENT (page 165): While thanking God for strengthening you, also consider and thank those in your community who share in your journey. This exercise inspires appreciation for cherished loved ones.

Dear Heavenly Father,

You want to sustain and strengthen us to manage this broken world. I praise You for strategically placing the friends and family members who share in healing my afflictions and I in theirs. You never intended for us to go it alone. May I always depend on You and also rely on those You gave me to walk this journey together with me.

In Jesus' name. Amen.

PART 2

PRACTICES for STRENGTH and HEALING

Knowing You Are Enough

USEFUL FOR: Giving yourself permission to consider and appreciate how God made you to be enough; helping you appreciate that God chooses to make you human; accepting both your strengths and weaknesses.

TIME: 10–15 minutes

OVERVIEW: In this exercise, imagine God's loving gaze upon you. When you envision and experience how God really views you with love and grace, you can appreciate how He made you.

INSTRUCTIONS:

1. Sit in a comfortable place that is free of distractions.

2. Consider the verse Psalm 18:19b as it appears in the New Living Translation (NLT): "He delights in me."

3. Close your eyes, and envision the Lord here with you right now. Imagine He is gazing upon you with delight.

4. Ask Him to make this visual clear if there are obstacles in the way, such as negative self-talk or a false belief of unworthiness. Maybe bring to mind how Jesus welcomed the children, as you are His child.

5. Stay with this visual as long as necessary to gain a felt sense of "being enough" in His gaze. This visualization exercise will have a lasting impact if you not only think it but also viscerally experience it.

6. Carry the verse forward as a daily mantra—*He delights in me*—noticing how it impacts you and how you feel about yourself.

7. Recall this feeling of being enough whenever you feel uncertain or are facing insecurities or challenging circumstances.

Dwelling in God's Safety

USEFUL FOR: Bringing you an internal sense of safety and security when you need it most, instead of looking to others to provide a sense of safety or security, which can leave you vulnerable. This exercise focuses on an internal sense of God's safety and security, which you carry around and can access regularly.

TIME: 5–10 minutes

OVERVIEW: When you struggle to sleep or find rest due to an unsettled feeling, shift to peace of mind by recalling that God promises to keep your soul safe—you know that in your gut.

INSTRUCTIONS:

1. As part of your bedtime routine or when you seek rest, bring this verse to mind: "In peace I will both lie down and sleep, for You alone, Lord, have me dwell in safety" (Psalm 4:8). Write it down on a piece of paper and tape it to your bedside.

2. Start by reciting the second part of the verse: "For You alone, Lord, have me dwell in safety."

3. Progressively relax your body muscles, slowly from head to toe, as you release the effort to your Heavenly Father who compels you dwell in His safe and capable hands.

4. Take a deep breath and then exhale, before finishing the verse: "In peace I will both lie down and sleep."

5. Repeat as many times as you need for your mind and body to settle into His Spirit.

Basking in the Freedom of God

USEFUL FOR: When you feel powerless and without choice.

TIME: 15–20 minutes

OVERVIEW: You first need to be filled by Him to have anything worthwhile to give to others, so you will sit with Him and then consider your choices. What are you willing to release to others?

INSTRUCTIONS:

1. Grab your journal, and find a place where you can be curious with yourself in God's presence.

2. Close your eyes and ask God to help you surrender to His love. Try to release all effort and envision resting in His loving arms.

3. Open your eyes and make a list of any obligatory thoughts that interrupted your focus on God—thoughts that start with "I should" or "I have to."

4. Review your list and consider which "shoulds" are not your responsibility. Cross those off your list, praying for God to handle each responsibility that isn't yours ("making sure my husband makes it to his weekly men's group").

5. Then, consider which "shoulds" or "ought to's" are more about pleasing or being admired by others. This week when you serve others, make conscious choices and allow that freedom for others as well.

6. Last, consider what you are willing or want to do—and that you feel God gives you strength and energy for—and prioritize those things this week.

The Power of Influence

USEFUL FOR: When struggling with a sense of powerlessness in a relationship or seeking to let go of control of another person; examining more closely the idea of influence versus control in relationships.

TIME: 20–30 minutes

OVERVIEW: Take a closer look at your dearest relationships and consider how you might better impact them with the love of God. Examine how much power or influence you have—and are susceptible to—in your relationships. Ultimately, bettering your relationship dynamics comes from receiving and extending true Christian love.

INSTRUCTIONS:

1. Grab a blank piece of paper and a few different-colored writing utensils.

2. Draw in the middle of the paper a circle, and write your name and the name of God that best reflects your surrendered relationship with Him. For me, I surrender best when I think of God as my Abba Father, so that's the name I use.

3. Next, write the names of the people you are most connected to or desire to be connected to, and circle those names.

4. Draw arrows pointing to the names, with the thickness indicating how much influence or control you try to exert toward them.

5. Draw a parallel line and arrow pointing back to your name with the appropriate thickness on how much influence you allow them in your life.

6. Step back and notice the patterns.

7. Prayerfully consider adjustments God wants to make in your relationships, whether that means seeking less influence or control, or taking in more or less influence and letting go to God.

To Control . . . Or Not to Control?

USEFUL FOR: Getting your mind and heart aligned when you feel unsettled and tempted to control something outside of yourself to gain what can only be a false sense of peace or security.

TIME: 15–30 minutes

OVERVIEW: Understanding what is in your control and what is not shows spiritual maturity.

INSTRUCTIONS:

1. Find a quiet place to sit with a journal.

2. Take a few good deep breaths to settle your body, and find a comfortable position.

3. Ask God to meet you exactly where you are in mind, body, and soul. Ask Him to show you evidence of His loving-kindness toward you—this could be an image or a feeling in your body. Or just mindfully recall His care for you.

4. Write in your journal, speaking to God about what may be unsettling or on your mind right now.

5. Pause after pouring your thoughts and feelings onto the paper, and again ask Him to show you His loving-kindness toward you.

6. Acknowledge what is not in your control but is in His hands, such as other peoples' feelings or a situational outcome, and prayerfully ask Him to deepen your trust in Him.

7. Then be mindful of what is in your control, such as your thoughts, behaviors, and reactions, and pray for God's grace in choosing your responses.

8. Journal about these insights, being honest in your thoughts, feelings, and desires, so that God's Spirit may effectively offer guidance.

9. Write down some action plans you might take. For example, are you in a push-pull pattern with a partner? How will you respond differently next time to break that pattern?

10. As you move through your daily life, continue to remind yourself that you have control only over your own actions and thoughts, and humbly acknowledge that God can handle the rest—far better than you ever could.

Allowing Your Emotions

USEFUL FOR: When you consistently don't allow yourself to experience the full range of emotions God created in you, this exercise can help you sort out those feelings. In this exercise, you practice connecting with your emotions while in the presence of a Heavenly Father who promises to comfort and see you through. You will identify your emotions, and what you may be subconsciously believing or doing in relation to those feelings.

TIME: 15–30 minutes

OVERVIEW: When stuck in the codependence dance, you might not even be able to put words to your emotions—let alone recognize the solutions God has at the ready for you. Maybe you feel intimidated by your emotional energy or confused as to how to process uncomfortable feelings. For example, when you stifle your anger you might find that the emotion comes out in passive-aggressive ways. What we don't realize is that anger can actually be a useful emotion—to give us the energy needed to say "no" or to set a boundary for ourselves.

INSTRUCTIONS:

Find a comfortable place to journal. Start your journal by writing a letter to God. The letter will include the following:

- *What am I feeling?* Are you angry, sad, lonely, scared, embarrassed, or confused, currently or in recent days (see the Emotions Chart on page 170). Notice these are feelings, not thoughts.

- *What do I normally do when I feel this way?* ("I might hold my tongue, but nonverbally I am seething and holding my jaw tight, short with everyone around me.") Ask God to show you a better way to release these emotions (for example, scream into a pillow until you feel release of that emotional energy).

- Ask God's forgiveness for any actions you feel ashamed of due to your emotions coming out sideways—such as expressing your feelings inappropriately or misdirecting your anger at an innocent party who happens to be in the line of fire.

- Continue the letter by telling Him what you seek out or feel you need from Him, yourself, and others in order for you to achieve a calmer disposition.

- Share with God something you need to be able to say "no" to or a personal boundary you'd like to establish.

- Or share with God if you want to say "yes" to something that would be healthy for you in growing closer to God and interdependently with others. Maybe you want to stretch yourself to take a healthy step toward deeper relationship.

- Ask God in your letter if He has a truth He wants to share with you. Stay in conversation with God until you know what you may emotionally need to help you shift these feelings into something that fills you with satisfaction or appreciation. Refer to the Relations and Needs Chart (page 171) and see what jumps off the page.

- Close the letter by thanking God for meeting you in this place, and ask Him to give you the courage to act in a way that is in alignment with what He just showed you in this time.

Pinpointing Emotional and Relational Needs

USEFUL FOR: When you don't find purpose in connecting to your emotions or when you get stuck in your emotions. When you find your emotions interrupt your ability to assess and ask for what you really need and how you want to move forward in relationships with God, self, and others. When you try many things to feel better but nothing seems to work.

TIME: 20–30 minutes

OVERVIEW: Emotions help you identify, label, feel, and express your needs. There are no shortcuts. By working through your emotions, you can know and therefore reach, grasp, and attain your God-given needs.

INSTRUCTIONS:

1. Find a quiet space where you can be with God.

2. Sit quietly and go inward to your heart and your body sensations while prayerfully asking God to make His presence known to you.

3. Label what you may be feeling inside, and reveal it to God. Ask God to help you experience this feeling enough to give expression to it—crying, shaking, screaming into a pillow, or whatever helps you release your emotions.

4. Notice if the physical release satiates the feeling a bit. Relax into this for a moment before moving on to the next step.

5. After you have allowed the emotions to move through you, reflect on what needs may be underlying your emotions. If you draw a blank, see the Relations and Needs Chart (page 171).

6. Once you have strongly identified a need, ask God to help you fulfill this need through Him or to bring forward a memory of a time when He met this or a similar need.

7. Consider people in your life to whom you could reach out and make a request for your need to be met interdependently ("I know we both work hard for our family. I'm feeling unappreciated lately when I don't get a lot of thank you's. Do you mind letting me know you appreciate me?").

8. Ask God to ground you in the fact that He will always meet you in your needs, sometimes calling on other people and often through His Spirit.

Fine-Tuning Your Expectations

USEFUL FOR: When you have expectations but continually get disappointed and struggle to accept that others won't or can't meet them. When you need to take a closer look at your true needs and what is motivating your expectations.

TIME: 10–20 minutes

OVERVIEW: You will spend time journaling about your expectations of others, or maybe of yourself, and shift the expectation to include a foundation of freedom. Acknowledging your need or desire is a vulnerable yet freeing and respectful place to speak from. This is a space that allows another to be honest with their "yes" or "no." When you hear a "no," you may feel disappointment and even despair. Yet Jesus is near and you can sit at His feet to allow Him to minister to your soul and meet your need in another way. Consider the healthy interdependence that can grow in this place where you allow yourself to be true about your motivation and invite others to be themselves.

INSTRUCTIONS:

1. Journal about a disappointment you may be experiencing in a relationship.

2. Sit quietly, and then ask God to show you what emotional need you are trying to get met. (Refer to the Relations and Needs Chart on page 171 if necessary to assist you in accurately identifying your emotions and needs.)

3. Return to your journal, and rewrite your expectation as a request: "Would you be willing to . . . ?"

4. Ask God for the strength and courage to go back into this relationship with a request, not an expectation.

5. Ask God to give you the ability to tolerate the answer, whether it is "yes" or "no" from this other person.

6. Intentionally go to this person with your specific request, knowing God can uphold you even when you are disappointed.

God to the Rescue!

USEFUL FOR: Helping you stay in your own lane while alongside others versus trying to rescue them from feeling tough challenges; breaking patterns of enabling.

TIME: 15–30 minutes

OVERVIEW: Ultimately, you want to grow your trust in how God plans to work through others' experiences. In this exercise, you will walk through a verbal and physical dialogue, releasing trust to God and acknowledging that only He can rescue and save others. This does not apply to occasionally lending a helping hand or being in kind service to others.

INSTRUCTIONS:

1. Find a quiet space where you are free from distractions and can focus on just yourself and God.

2. Consider any efforts you are possibly making to rescue or save another person, such as regularly giving them money or habitually excusing their unsavory behavior without even having a conversation.

3. Surrender any such enabling or dismissive behaviors to the Lord. Do that by envisioning yourself taking the person by the hand and walking them over to the Lord. Or use an object that represents that person, such as a token or photo, and place it in a small box labeled "Yours," to feel the experience of letting go and letting God.

4. Pray in gratitude to God for being this person's Savior, and thank Him for releasing you of the burden you have felt. Now, trust that He has taken it up.

5. Knowing that God plans to divinely guide this person's life, ask Him also for guidance in yours to show you how to best be in relationship with this person without taking the weight of their behaviors on your back again.

6. Pay special attention to the difference you feel in your body when you give this person to God, so you can recall and come back to this memory anytime you are tempted in the future to come to someone's rescue.

But First . . . Your Emotional Wellness

USEFUL FOR: Resolving conflict with someone you love; dealing with feelings of abandonment or resentment that loved ones are emotionally unavailable when you need them. Recognizing you have a God who is on your side always—even when you are in the wrong. This sense of not feeling alone and being "fought for" can be a lifesaver in relaxing the hyper-defensiveness that fuels codependency.

TIME: 15–25 minutes

OVERVIEW: This exercise reinforces that God wants to meet your needs and empower you to be in relationship with a renewed spirit. He can be "your help and your shield," especially in times of conflict. You will envision the many attributes of God and notice what you need most from Him and others at this time. You will share with God your deepest thoughts, beliefs, and feelings, inviting His love to move through you before you seek to resolve a conflict.

INSTRUCTIONS:

1. Find a comfortable place to sit quietly with God, maybe even in your car for a few moments after dropping the kids off at school or before work.

2. Envision God, knowing He sees you as well. He witnesses what you are going through, so cry out to Him, even if it's without words.

3. Ask God to fill you with His presence in whatever way you most need Him right now.

4. Recall memories of when God has met you in this way or worked through other people to inspire in you a sense of fulfillment.

5. Once you feel you have allowed God to meet you in this need and feel a sense of fulfillment, only *then* try to repair a conflict.

6. Start by asking the person with whom you are in conflict: "When is the best time for us to talk through what happened?" Be sure to give both of you the time needed to be prepared for such a discussion.

7. Consider jotting down what you want to say when you meet, always starting by recognizing your part in the conflict ("I apologize for assuming and accusing you of not caring for me when you didn't respond to me this morning").

8. To reconcile, speak truth with love and grace, perhaps even sharing ways to find relational interdependence.

Letting God Take Inventory

USEFUL FOR: When you feel troubled about a relationship and need direction on how to move forward with greater focus on interdependence. When you recognize that your past may be casting a shadow over how you experience your present. When you have consistent conflicts with multiple people in your life or are regularly let down.

TIME: 20–40 minutes

OVERVIEW: When you are in a relational conflict, it is best to look at the log in your own eye (Matthew 7:3), before seeking to resolve a conflict with someone. You will sit quietly to let God take your inventory, gently receiving His correction and guidance. God's mercy is always sufficient and can shore you up enough to feel secure in accepting responsibility for your part in relationship conflicts.

INSTRUCTIONS:

1. Bring your Bible to a quiet space where you can hear from God, free from distractions.

2. Read this verse slowly: "Search me, God, and know my heart" (Psalm 139:23).

3. Take a few moments to open yourself to the Lord, maybe assuming an open posture that embodies your willingness to hear from Him.

4. Continue praying the second part of the verse (Verse 24): "Put me to the test and know my anxious thoughts; and see if there is any hurtful way in me."

5. Sit openly, allowing God to bring to your mind or heart anything He wants you to focus on. Breathe mindfully, and stay open to whatever pops up in your thoughts or spirit.

6. Allow God to gently minister to you through His Holy Spirit.

7. Before leaving this time of meditation, ask the Lord to lead you in the everlasting way and consider what He may be asking you to do going forward.

8. As you move on with your day, consider how you can put into action what the Lord shares with you.

Empowerment, Courtesy of God

USEFUL FOR: When you have given a relationship your best efforts, and yet it doesn't seem to be working. When you feel broken and confused and need to feel seen by God for all that you are experiencing. When you need hope and empowerment to keep moving toward interdependence.

TIME: 10–15 minutes

OVERVIEW: Take full advantage of your freedom in Christ by sharing with God *all* that you are feeling and experiencing. Drop the niceties or "supposed to's," and really be honest with God—He knows anyway. By being brutally honest is a show of great faith because you trust God is big enough to love and support you no matter what. In this exercise, the only rule is to be truthful with God and be open to His response to you.

INSTRUCTIONS:

1. This exercise is about using your imagination. First, release any internal voices, and share your thoughts and feelings with God—nothing is off-limits. He already sees you.

2. Grab your journal if you prefer to communicate with Him through written words, or find a place where you can speak as loudly or as quietly as you desire and talk to Him.

3. Freely share with Him what is on your heart and mind—whether it's an angry outburst or an expression of passion. Don't stop until you have exhausted *all* you wanted to say or express.

4. Once you have said all you have to say, take a few deep breaths, breathing in the Holy Spirit.

5. Sit quietly and ask God to respond to you in a way that is most accessible to you—maybe this will be through inspired thoughts or words that come up, or He will send messages in dreams or visions.

6. Allow yourself to envision even pushing Him away if this is how you feel, recognizing that He will allow you to do this, and yet He will still lovingly show patience until you are ready for Him to comfort you.

7. Consider the possibility that you might be taking out on God your feelings about a certain person. Envision this person in the room, and notice if you can now hear anything different from God.

8. Possibly journal about this experience, noticing what may need to be cleared out of the way so you can fully experience His love and compassion for you.

9. If this is too difficult to untangle, consider talking with a spiritual director, minister, or counselor about your conflict.

Shove Off, Shame!

USEFUL FOR: When you feel down on yourself, agitated, or particularly unsettled—you may be struggling with shame. When you hesitate or have a hard time seeing your fault in relational interactions—shame could be the trickster that deceives.

TIME: 10–15 minutes

OVERVIEW: Shame at its extreme can trick you into believing you are bad, unacceptable, unlovable, and a multitude of other lies that keep you emotionally isolated and self-critical. Shame tends to be such a heavy emotion that it steals your identity in Christ, perpetuating unhealthy feelings and behaviors. Jesus was known for "despising the shame" (Hebrews 12:2) and took it all upon Himself so we can live! This exercise emphasizes these truths and puts shame in its rightful place.

INSTRUCTIONS:

1. Whatever mindset you are in at this moment, pause and thank Jesus Christ for taking away *all* of your sin and shame. He gives you instead a place at His table, calling you friend (Luke 5:20).

2. Think on this for a moment, really taking it in to your mind, heart, and soul that He does not feel ashamed of you. Rather, He loves you just as you are—especially perhaps in your messiness, because that's where you humble yourself before Him.

3. As you move through your week, consider what could be different today, knowing you are deeply and completely loved by the Creator, who knows everything—and I mean *everything*— about you.

4. Ask Him for the courage to walk in His love and to live according to your values in Him.

5. Shame can be one of the sharpest arrows of the enemy. Please consider talking with a trusted friend, pastor, or counselor if you have trouble shaking off feelings of shame.

A Stronghold on Boundaries

USEFUL FOR: When you feel uncertain or too easily swayed by others, not focused on what God is doing in you. When you feel bulldozed or taken advantage of, or when you focus more on wanting the other person to understand your needs versus taking mindful steps to let God protect you.

TIME: 20–30 minutes

OVERVIEW: You will welcome God to examine your heart through a contemplative exercise, and then you will seek to hold a solid boundary throughout the week, even when faced with situations that normally sway you.

INSTRUCTIONS:

1. Spend time in prayer, asking God to show you where or with whom you want to develop more interdependence.

2. Ask God to show you how you are separate and solid from this individual and what you have to offer that relationship by staying connected to who He made you to be.

3. Find a sense of clarity about your solidness, your edges, even feeling into where your physical edges (skin and clothes) end and that person's begin.

4. Staying connected to yourself and the Holy Spirit in you, notice how God fills you all the way to the edges, where your physicality ends and the air around you begins.

5. Stand in this territory God gave you, this temple He made, and the gifts and purposes He inspires in you specifically.

6. Next time you meet with this person or run into a situation that can sway you, use this felt sense of clarity about your physical edges to support your steadfast spirit or sense of boundary.

Relying on God as Your Rock

USEFUL FOR: When you feel lost or alone, maybe even forgotten. When you define yourself more based on what other people think of you than on the truth of who you are as God's creation.

TIME: 5–10 minutes

OVERVIEW: This exercise helps you recognize God's constant presence with you. You will experience Him as your rock and the one who will always sustain you, as long as you allow Him. When we understand His solidness, you feel your own strength and can be more decisive in your relationships instead of feeling wishy-washy and tossed around like a wave. When grounded and rooted in Christ, you realize you are enough—but still with freedom to grow. From this place of understanding, you better relate to God, yourself, and others.

INSTRUCTIONS:

1. No matter where you are, take a few deep breaths and consider this verse: "I will never desert you, nor will I ever abandon you" (Hebrews 13:5).

2. Take a moment to envision God with you. You might perceive Him as a mist in the air or a tangible figure. Maybe recall a picture you have seen of His image, or just sense His presence in your spirit.

3. Take a few deep breaths, exhaling slowly, as you ask God to help you experience His solidness, love, and care. Imagine sitting at His feet, on His lap, or beside Him.

4. Pray that He instill a felt sense that you can trust He will sustain you and help you through any situation that is on your mind. Acknowledge that He is sustaining you *right now* just through your breath.

Moderation in Matters of the Heart

USEFUL FOR: When you are not allowing others to positively influence you. When you are overly influenced by others. When you need to find a sense of safety and protection after feeling repeatedly wounded.

TIME: 15–20 minutes

OVERVIEW: You will prayerfully ask God to guide you in a practice of protecting your heart, while balancing that with openness of the heart In all matters, you want to seek moderation.

INSTRUCTIONS:

1. Take a moment to think of a specific relationship you want to improve.

2. Prayerfully ask God to meet you with kindness, grace, and strength to face what He may want to show you.

3. Ask God to help you see if you over- or under-protect yourself in this relationship.

4. Notice a word or visual that grabs your mind's attention, allowing the Holy Spirit to speak to you, even if it doesn't seem to make sense right now.

5. While in this contemplative prayer, lay one hand protectively over your heart and the other openly extended to receive.

6. Notice how this posture feels, shifting from right to left if necessary for you to feel more comfortable—or you might even prefer to put both hands out or both over your heart. Play around with it. Ask God to show you the posture most needed in this relationship to help you stay attuned to His Spirit.

7. Before ending this time of prayer and reflection, ask God to continually fill you with faith that He is always the protector of your soul and to give you courage to boldly navigate your human relationships.

Being Responsible "To" Versus "For"

USEFUL FOR: When you take too much responsibility for people and circumstances you can't control. When you find you apologize when no fault or blame is necessary.

TIME: 15–30 minutes

OVERVIEW: Sometimes as children, we were given more responsibility than was developmentally appropriate, like my dear friend who was responsible for preparing all her own meals by age seven. Other times, we thought it was our responsibility to keep our caregivers happy because their moods seemed to depend on our behaviors. Whatever the source, maybe you learned to take on responsibilities you aren't qualified to handle or have no control over, such as other people's emotions. In this exercise you will examine what is your responsibility based on the roles God grants you so you can release to Him what is *not* yours to carry.

INSTRUCTIONS:

1. Prayerfully consider a relationship in which you take on too much responsibility. Maybe this is based on how much effort or emotional energy this relationship takes, or perhaps it's a relationship you try to avoid because it feels burdensome.

2. Make a list of things you feel responsible for in this relationship.

3. Invite God to review your list with you and consider what you actually have control over ("I can give positive feedback or affirmation to my friend") and what you don't ("I can't force my friend to feel confident—confidence is an inside job").

4. Review your list again and consider your role in this relationship. Journal about how you can more effectively fulfill that role ("I can be supportive in this friendship, but it is not my role to ensure or even worry about my friend's career success").

5. Review your list once again and make tweaks that put into action your support versus your rescue ("I can suggest revisions to improve my friend's résumé, but drafting their cover letter or completing their employment applications for them is crossing a line").

6. Contemplate these statements that clearly define how you are responsible in your relationships. Call on the Lord, release this person to His loving care, and wait on Him to reveal how you can be a support.

Aligning with Jesus

USEFUL FOR: When you are closed off and feeling a lack of connection to others. When you are overly connected to others and feel overwhelmed, sometimes taking on their experiences as your own, therefore trying to control something you can't control.

TIME: as much time as you need

OVERVIEW: You will follow Jesus' model of allowing yourself to join and attune to what others are experiencing. He models for you the depth of that connection in relationship.

INSTRUCTIONS:

1. Sit prayerfully with the Lord, asking Him to bring to your mind and heart someone who needs to connect with you today.

2. Ask the Lord to soften your heart and its protective layer until you feel *with* this other person's experience while also maintaining a healthy sense of being separate from them.

3. Ask the Lord to help you be present and not go in with a "fix" when you reach out to this person.

4. If the person wants to share, silently offer a listening ear and heartfelt compassion.

5. Notice how the connection grows from empathy.

Allowing Scripture to Be Personal and Powerful

USEFUL FOR: When you feel weak, uncertain, intimidated, or even scared to take new steps toward interdependency. When you need a jolt of God's strength, love, and guidance to help direct your thoughts and behaviors to fresh, healthier ways.

TIME: 10–15 minutes

OVERVIEW: You will meditate on the scripture below while thinking of the situation in which you want to act differently, so you can move forward with greater intention and courage.

INSTRUCTIONS:

1. Find a quiet and comfortable place to sit mindfully and in contemplation. Take a few deep breaths to settle in.

2. In your journal or on a piece of paper, write a personalized version of 2 Timothy 1:7: "For God has not given us a spirit of timidity, but of power and love and discipline." A personalized version may go something like this: "God, You did not give me a spirit of fear or timidness, but You gave me a Spirit of empowerment, love, and self-control."

3. Repeat your version to yourself at least three times, and notice any shifts in your posture, breathing, core, or emotional state.

4. Ask God to help you maintain this new sense of strength as you consider the relationships you hope to face with greater confidence.

Letting Go and Letting God

USEFUL FOR: When you feel anxious, unsettled, or in need. When your world feels anything but peaceful.

TIME: 10–20 minutes

OVERVIEW: You will spend time praying and making practical the verses from Philippians 4, allowing God to bring His peace. This may take the form of a direction for your behavior, or it may be supernatural and not require any action on your part at all. You will allow God to do His part, as you do yours: bring your heart of gratitude and express your needs.

INSTRUCTIONS:

1. Find a quiet place to spend time with God in prayer.

2. Read Philippians 4:5b–7: "The Lord is near. Do not be anxious about anything, but in everything by prayer and pleading with thanksgiving let your requests be made known to God. And the peace of God, which surpasses all comprehension, will guard your hearts and your minds in Christ Jesus."

3. Focus on the first part: "The Lord is near." Sit with this realization until you agree to allow His presence to be with you. He is already near, so it's really about acknowledging this even in the midst of distractions.

4. "With thanksgiving let your requests be made known to God." Moving on, consider and express your gratitude for God's influence in your life and in your relationships. You are training your brain to see the positive intention on your part.

5. Still in gratitude, express your needs or wants to God. "Be anxious for nothing." Boldly make all requests without holding back.

6. Sit quietly, and notice any prompts from God. Has the energy of your body, mind, or spirit shifted? How so? Consider journaling about it.

7. Offer appreciation for God's gifts to you. "Peace . . . which surpasses all comprehension, will guard your hearts."

Replenishment through Soul-Care

USEFUL FOR: When you want to care well for others but just don't seem to have the patience, energy, or motivation due to your own empty tank.

TIME: 15 minutes minimum—can spend more time if you want to get real creative

OVERVIEW: This is a fun exercise that inspires you to treat yourself as you want to treat others—with love and care. You will make a "soul-care" jar filled with activities you can do to refill your tank. You will consider various areas of your soul-care—spiritual, emotional, physical, and relational. In these categories, you'll identify activities you love or wish to try.

INSTRUCTIONS:

1. Gather four different-colored pens or pencils, and at least twenty-four scraps of paper.

2. Assign each color of pen or pencil to one of these four categories: spiritual, emotional, physical, and relational.

3. For each category, write six ways (on six individual paper scraps) that you would like to give yourself a little dose of loving care. For example, you might write "twenty minutes of meditation at the park" (spiritual). Or to lift your moods, give yourself "permission to watch a funny or sentimental movie" (emotional). For relationship health, you'd love to "invite friends over for game night" (relational).

4. After writing your self-love wish-list items onto the pieces of paper, fold them, and drop them into your jar.

5. Now here's the best part! When you randomly need a show of self-love, pluck a piece of paper out of the jar and partake in whatever activity got picked: "treat myself to a hot stone massage" (physical).

Getting into Harmony

USEFUL FOR: When you have no words left to pray and yet desperately want to follow God. When taking steps toward healthier relationships and finding you can still feel hurt and disappointment; although this is a normal part of the journey, you might need your chin to be lifted to God's greater promise. This exercise is useful to allow His Spirit to attune to you.

TIME: 10 minutes

OVERVIEW: Sometimes you might just be too weary to put words to your needs. You might find such days are well spent allowing God's love and care to wash over you through song. There are many artists I turn to for this, as I may need a specific type of song that acknowledges my humanity at that point—one that speaks to my pain or anguish. Some of my favorite musicians are Lauren Daigle, Hillary Scott & The Scott Family, Ben and Noelle Kilgore, Steffany Gretzinger, and JJ Heller. You can choose one of these artists or choose your own mix of music that speaks to your soul.

INSTRUCTIONS:

1. Find a private spot and grab your streaming device. Pull up a song, such as "Thy Will" by Hillary Scott & The Scott Family, or one of your favorites.

2. Consider the lyrics as you relax your body and bring it to a comfortably open posture.

3. Allow yourself to cry out in anguish or joy as it authentically arises.

4. Listen to the song as many times as it feels inspiring.

5. Allow yourself to land on the truth that He sees you, hears you, and has plans of goodness for you.

Growing Your Blessings

USEFUL FOR: When you feel emotionally stuck. When you can't get over or reconcile a hardship from the past. When you have already taken action toward elements you can control but struggle to let go of what you can't control.

TIME: 5–10 minutes

OVERVIEW: Focus on utilizing the resources and people God places in your path to help you grow closer to Him. This exercise motivates you to grow in your spiritual and relational maturity.

INSTRUCTIONS:

1. In your prayer time, thank God specifically for the people in your life who inspire you to move forward, encourage you, and help you grow toward God. Ask God to bring to your mind a person in your sphere with whom He especially wants you to grow a greater kinship.

2. Visualize a forward path that God has laid out for you. It could be a few feet ahead, or it might look like a long highway. Notice the light He bestows upon that path—and potentially the people He places on it.

3. If you currently feel lost in the desert, you are in good company. As did the Israelites, trust that your land of milk and honey lies ahead (Deuteronomy 27:3).

4. Make efforts this week to re-envision this path and connect with the people God has chosen to sojourn with you.

Being Reliant, Not Dependent

USEFUL FOR: Finding the balanced characteristics of interdependence in relationships. Better understanding patterns of independence and codependence.

TIME: 15–30 minutes

OVERVIEW: God is your source, your sustainer. While you always have Him to depend on, He built you to have relationships with others—and that includes your relationship to self. This exercise guides you to find balance in your relationships by committing time in contemplation with God and then reaching out to those with whom you are in close relationship.

INSTRUCTIONS:

1. Grab your journal, and go to a quiet place where you can be introspective. Maybe even go outdoors to a peaceful spot.

2. Start with a moment of stillness, taking deep breaths—breathing God in and breathing all mental distractions out.

3. Consider if there is a particular person you tend to depend on too much or ask God to reveal if you tend to be too independent and not ask for emotional help.

4. Thank Him that He has gifted people to meet your needs at times, yet recognizing that God sometimes works alone.

5. Lastly, consider the challenges of others as well. Send messages of inspiration or call to offer support or lend an ear. Healthy relationships are mutually loving and respectful.

Love as the Motivator

USEFUL FOR: Getting to know yourself and being honest in God's presence. When you feel accused of things you don't recognize or believe to be true.

TIME: 20–30 minutes

OVERVIEW: You will spend time in God's presence to take an honest look at whether your motives match your behaviors. Standing in God's grace, you will be able to own behaviors or attitudes perhaps you didn't want to admit. As God already knows everything and loves us unconditionally, you will grow in courage and learn to align your motivations and behaviors. Too often, fear of judgment from God impedes our motivation to truly love and serve another.

INSTRUCTIONS:

1. Grab your journal and find a place with no distractions that feels comforting to you.

2. Sit with God in this quiet place, thanking Him that He loves you wider, longer, deeper, and harder than anyone on this earth ever could (Ephesians 3:17–19).

3. Acknowledge that He alone knows *everything* about you—past, present, and future.

4. Ask Him to help you take an honest, grace-based look at any unhealthy patterns of behavior you exhibit in your relationships.

5. In looking at this behavior, ascertain your motivations by asking yourself the following questions:

    - *What am I trying to get out of this situation?*
    - *What do I ultimately desire from this relationship?*
    - *What am I hiding about myself?*
    - *What am I scared may happen?*

6. Notice if your behavior patterns reflect the answers to your questions in an obvious way. Ask God to show you how to be honest with yourself and others, while "being rooted and grounded in love"—the love of Christ (Ephesians 3:17).

7. Share humbly with your loved ones what God has shared with you. With the exception of when in an abusive relationship, being vulnerable with those you love can deepen your relational bonds.

Seek and Find Relationship Satisfaction

USEFUL FOR: When you feel taken advantage of in relationships. When you are seeking or engaging in a relationship only because you need something from the other person.

TIME: 15–30 minutes or take small moments over a few days

OVERVIEW: You will sit with curiosity and write out what you give and what you get from specific relationships. Then you will examine how you might better serve someone without losing yourself, as well as look at healthy ways to elicit respect from others.

INSTRUCTIONS:

1. Grab your journal and pen and find a quiet place to contemplate.

2. Pray that God will help you see clearly, with His ever-present mercy, what you give and what you get from a relationship you are concerned about at this time.

3. Record your insights in your journal. For example, you might write, "I give a lot of time volunteering at the church, but then in private I often complain about it. Maybe my giving is really about getting a reputation as a good Christian, not about wanting to contribute out of love."

4. Ask God to help you receive from Him how to best treat this relationship: "Lord, do I need to shift my attentions so that I'm giving in the spirit of love? Or do I need to donate less time and take better care of myself? Please guide me to the giving opportunities that best fit into my schedule and meet my soul's purpose."

5. For the rest of this week, fully trust that God will not leave you (or anyone else) stranded in your dilemma. He will offer the perfect solution, for all involved, to your relationship problem.

EMOTIONS CHART

Rage	Anger	Annoyance
Despair	Sadness	Melancholy
Terror	Fear	Worry
Self-Contempt	Shame	Embarrassment
Joy	Happiness	Contentment
Bravery	Empowerment	Confidence
Surprise	Confusion	Curiosity
Powerlessness	Defeat	Humility

RELATIONS AND NEEDS CHART

To have limits & boundaries	To be delighted in	Acknowledgment & support
Nurturance & comfort	Kindness & love	To be known
To be playful & explore	Safety & security	To be valued & accepted
Healthy touch & affection	Autonomy & privacy	Understanding & empathy
Affirmation & appreciation	To be believed & believed in	Patience & recognition of humanity
To be heard	To feel & express emotions	To belong & to be part of a collective

ACKNOWLEDGMENTS

I am humbled and beyond grateful that the Lord gave me this experience to share all that He has taught me over the years. Thank you, Lord, for entrusting me with Your Word. May only that which is of You be comprehended and all else fall away.

I owe a huge amount of my learning and gratitude to my past and present clients, who have allowed me to walk in these sacred places with them.

My husband, Trevor, has been a champion of my seeking the Lord since he first shared the good news with me while we were dating. Had God not used Trevor's gentle and beautiful spirit to influence me, I may have floundered in my unhealthy patterns for many more years than I did. Growing in our love for God and each other has been one of the greatest joys of my life. Thank you, my love.

To my Sisters at Heart, Kristen and Karen; and my most valued soul sisters, Blanca and Bonnie—you all inspire me to live more fully in the love of God, to risk vulnerability, and take steps toward owning my humanity. Thank you for always being there to cheer me on toward the most fulfilling love story I could ever dream up.

To one of my newest friends, Susann: how God placed us together still amazes me. I love that He built a truly interdependent relationship between us from the start. Your support and willingness to make sacrifices to allow me time to write leaves me eternally grateful.

To my Bible study friends who read my manuscript and gave me feedback—and have been all-around great cheerleaders along the way—thank you!

To those friends and family members who have taught me so much about myself and relationships, I appreciate the time we've had and even the hurts that helped me grow.

I also want to recognize my literary, professional, and spiritual mentors who are part of my journey and growth toward greater Christian love.

Last but not least, to the editors and staff at Zeitgeist for choosing me for this project and for being so kind, patient, and helpful as I moved through the process of writing my first devotional. I look forward to where God will lead me next.

REFERENCES

Sacred Companions: The Gift of Spiritual Friendship and Direction by David G. Benner

The Intimacy Factor, The Ground Rules for Overcoming the Obstacles of Truth, Respect and Lasting Love by Pia Mellody

Boundaries: When to Say Yes, How to Say No to Take Control of Your Life (updated and expanded version) by Dr. Henry Cloud and Dr. John Townsend

ABOUT THE AUTHOR

 **Wendy Lehnertz, MAPC, LMFT,** has been practicing faith-integrated psychotherapy with individuals, couples, and adult families for the past twenty-one years. Wendy's passion is to help each individual feel their true worth and identity in Christ, as well as to help couples and families function and love one another from this secure place of knowing they are unconditionally loved. Wendy focuses on elements of the Christian walk, such as empowerment and attunement to his Holy Spirit, boundaries to maintain health and safety, and embodiment of the regulated peace He desires to give our body, mind, and soul.

Hi there,

We hope *Healing from Codependency* helped you.
If you have any questions or concerns about your book,
or have received a damaged copy, please contact
customerservice@penguinrandomhouse.com. We're
here and happy to help.

Also, please consider writing a review on your favorite
retailer's website to let others know what you thought
of the book.

Sincerely,

The Zeitgeist Team